Dana H. Allin

NATO's Balkan Interventions

Adelphi Paper 347

Oxford University Press, Great Clarendon Street, Oxford OX2 6DP
Oxford New York
Athens Auckland Bangkok Bombay Calcutta Cape Town
Dar es Salaam Delhi Florence Hong Kong Istanbul Karachi
Kuala Lumpur Madras Madrid Melbourne Mexico City
Nairobi Paris Singapore Taipei Tokyo Toronto
and associated companies in
Berlin Ibadan

Oxford is a trade mark of Oxford University Press

Published in the United States
by Oxford University Press Inc., New York

© The International Institute for Strategic Studies 2002

First published July 2002 by **Oxford University Press** for
The International Institute for Strategic Studies
Arundel House, 13–15 Arundel Street, Temple Place, London WC2R 3DX
www.iiss.org

Director John Chipman
Editor Mats R. Berdal
Assistant Editor Jill Dobson
Production Shirley Nicholls

British Library Cataloguing in Publication Data

ata available

ry of Congress Cataloguing in Publication Data

19-851676-2
7-932X

Contents

Maps

Introduction

On 11 September 2001, NATO officials in Brussels were discussing how to continue their third Balkans intervention. Compared to earlier NATO campaigns in Bosnia and Kosovo, this Macedonia deployment was a low-key affair, with some 4,000 British-led troops to supervise a disarmament process agreed to by Albanian rebels. But the previous wars in Kosovo, Bosnia and Croatia – demonstrating the bottomless possibilities of ethnic brutality – had cast a long shadow. The threat of war in Macedonia raised many familiar dilemmas; these involved the morality and wisdom of military intervention in other peoples' civil wars, the prospects and limits of nation-building in ethnically fractured societies, the appropriate balance of transatlantic roles and the operational coherence of an extended Western alliance.

In an instant on that Tuesday, the terrorist mass murders in New York and Washington transformed transatlantic priorities. It was commonplace – and intuitively compelling – to say that the destruction of the World Trade Center had changed everything. That cannot be literally true, of course, and even in the narrower field of transatlantic relations, old arrangements and commitments cannot simply be jettisoned. What *can* be stated with reasonable confidence, however, is that a line has been drawn under a decade in which the wars of Yugoslavia's collapse dominated the transatlantic security relationship. While NATO as an organisation may continue to devote much of its energies to maintaining Balkan stability, the attention of Western leaders will be elsewhere.

Map 1 Former Yugoslavia

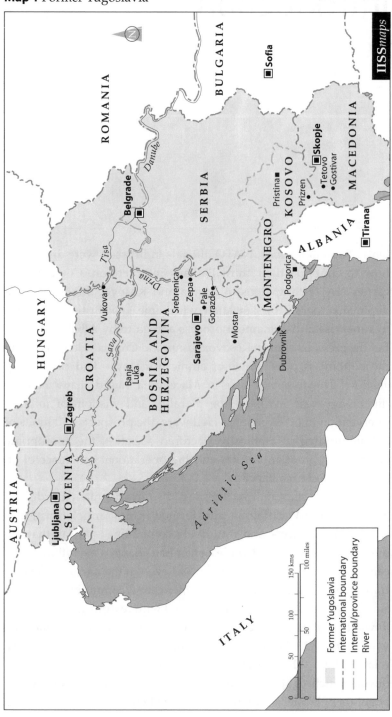

Yet Balkan instability retains the capacity to punish Western inattention, much as it did in the early 1990s. This makes it all the more important that alliance 'auto-pilot' settings be calibrated on the basis of sophisticated and not superficial lessons. This paper seeks to illuminate those lessons.

A Balkans learning curve

Even before Islamic terrorism had established itself, irrefutably, as a strategic-level threat, it seemed unlikely that Balkans crises could continue to dominate transatlantic relations so thoroughly as they did in the 1990s.

The decade-long Yugoslav crisis had two phases and two sorts of Western response. In the first phase, between 1990 and 1995, NATO as such only gradually became engaged. It was, in fact, the gradual, hesitant, unevenly distributed assumption of responsibilities in the face of a war of ethnic cleansing against Bosnia that caused much of the transatlantic rancour. The conflicts in Slovenia, Croatia and Bosnia did not directly threaten the core security of any NATO member state. Yet war in Europe, and especially war directed mainly against civilians, threatened the transatlantic values that were relatively more important to alliance cohesion now that the Soviet threat had disappeared. Increasingly bitter recriminations about where and how to draw the line against wartime atrocities underscored NATO's fragility. The divergence in views – especially between the United States on the one hand and Britain and France on the other – provoked a crisis of alliance relations reminiscent of the 1956 Suez debacle. As with Suez, there appeared to be fissures between New and Old World views that transcended – and even threatened to demolish – the idea of 'the West'.

The Bosnian war's corrosive effect on transatlantic unity was one important factor that led to a more effective American and NATO intervention in late 1995. Thereafter, in the second phase of the crisis, a determined effort was made to preserve alliance unity on Balkan matters. This effort was largely successful: chastened transatlantic partners had come to appreciate the high costs of disunity; and alliance perspectives on the moral and strategic challenge posed by Serbia's scorched-earth campaigns and, eventually, mass ethnic cleansing in Kosovo actually did converge. Convergence meant adopting common approaches to two kinds of dilemmas:

- first, concerning the wisdom and legitimacy of military intervention in complex ethno-national wars, i.e., the difficulties of taking sides and using force; and,

- second, the broader strategic choice – in a world rich in misery and humanitarian outrage – of *where* to intervene.

In an alliance marked by different attitudes towards the use of force, and different geopolitical interests and responsibilities, these two sets of dilemmas remain inherently divisive. Nonetheless, the Kosovo intervention was possible because the NATO allies united around some basic principles. They took sides in conflicts that were complicated, but far from morally opaque. They demonstrated the efficacy of using military force to defend human values and stability in a limited geographical space which can be roughly defined as Europe minus the former Soviet Union. And they assumed a long-term commitment to the management of at least two, and maybe three, Balkan protectorates.

Political leadership and ethnic conflict

The question of using force against the Serbs was the overriding source of alliance divisions during the war in Bosnia, and for that reason is the central focus here. This is not to suggest that outside military force can usefully be applied to all ethnic conflicts, or that Serbs have been responsible for all crimes in the wars of Yugoslavia's dissolution. The break-up of Yugoslavia – a disaster not necessarily finished by the year 2002 – has been a far more general trauma of ethno-national identity, demagoguery and fear. It was related to but not entirely dependent on policies promoted in Belgrade. Fear-mongering and ethnic cleansing were practised by Croats and, on a far smaller scale, Bosnian Muslims as well.[1] Kosovar Albanians have wrought their revenge in a low-intensity, but effective, wave of ethnic cleansing against the dwindling Serb minority in Kosovo. Macedonia's Slavic majority and Albanian minority have grown more bitterly resentful of one another and – despite moderate policies by successive governments in Skopje – have approached the edge of civil war. When the psychic shelter and, in many cases, political repression of a multinational federation such as Yugoslavia unravels, there does appear to be a dynamic that makes ethnic conflict likely, if not inevitable. Hans Morgenthau in 1957 took the

Balkan wars of the early twentieth century as his case in point to elucidate ethnic nationalism's inherent instabilities:

> *There are no inherent limits to the application of the principles of nationalism. If the peoples of Bulgaria, Greece, and Serbia could invoke those principles against Turkey, why could not the people of Macedonia invoke them against Bulgaria, Greece, and Serbia? ... Thus yesterday's oppressed cannot help becoming the oppressors of today because they are afraid lest they be again oppressed tomorrow.*[2]

The same dynamic was expressed vividly, if somewhat flippantly, by the economist Vladimir Gligorov (son of the former Macedonian president): 'Why should I be a minority in your state, when you can be a minority in mine?'.[3]

Still, as Morgenthau's example highlights, there are many places in post-communist Europe and, indeed, in the Balkans, where ethnic antagonisms and insecurities are real, memory of twentieth-century atrocities vivid – and yet, where horrors such as were visited upon the peoples of former Yugoslavia in the 1990s did *not* occur. As of early 2002, post-Yugoslav Macedonia itself was still a case of ethnic tensions being managed rather than fully unleashed. Other examples include the treatment of ethnic Turks in Bulgaria and ethnic Hungarians in Romania. What these examples suggest is that government policies and political leadership account for a great deal – probably most – of the difference between incipient ethnic conflict and murderous ethnic cleansing. In the case of Yugoslavia, one national leadership – indeed, one national leader – has been involved in all but one of the wars of ethnic cleansing since 1991. (The exception was the conflict between Croats and Bosnian Muslims from early 1993 until spring 1994, for which Croat nationalism and the nationalist leadership of Franjo Tudjman bear much of the blame.)

Argument in brief

This essay does not attempt to narrate or analyse the full range of Balkan engagements – economic, diplomatic and military – by Western powers and the United Nations since 1990. Rather, it focuses on three themes that divided the NATO allies, frequently – though by no means always – along transatlantic lines:

- *The use of military force.* Critics – frequently American critics – of the early, European-dominated response to Bosnia argued that the West's greatest Balkan error was a disinclination to use military force to stop the war against Bosnian civilians. (In practical terms, this meant military intervention against Serb forces, though the terrible record of Croat ethnic cleansing in central Bosnia and the Croatian Krajina was not ignored by the Americans.) This paper argues that the critics were largely right about this, something that the European allies came to acknowledge – at least implicitly – by the time of the Kosovo war.

- *The balancing* **of** *'exit strategies' against the need for a sustained and open-ended engagement.* Here it was Washington's European allies who got the better part of the argument – something that the new Republican administration in Washington has implicitly conceded, contrary to its earlier views. But that concession is compromised by the shock of 11 September, and the ensuing overriding demands on American energies and attention.

- *The problem of ethnic co-existence versus national self-determination in a multi-ethnic space.* Here the debate was less distinctly transatlantic, and the 'lessons' are far less clear. It is an unsolved problem that will continue to trouble the Atlantic alliance as it manages what are, in effect, international protectorates over Bosnia, Kosovo and, possibly in the future, Macedonia.

After the traumas inflicted upon these societies, it would be facile to suggest that the protecting powers can organise functioning states based on Western ideals of multi-ethnic tolerance any time in the foreseeable future. Even in Macedonia – long considered the notable success story among post-Yugoslav republics – ethnic tensions have lately been more salient than ethnic tolerance. Yet, it would be equally facile to suggest that the Western powers can afford to abandon those ideals altogether, or simply to walk away. NATO needs approaches that incorporate the lessons of its successes and failures, around which the transatlantic allies might reasonably hope – despite other pressing concerns – to stay engaged and stay united.

Chapter 1

Bosnia and the Transatlantic Problem

While the wars in Croatia and Kosovo troubled transatlantic relations, it was the war in Bosnia that most gravely threatened the alliance's fundamental consensus. Bosnia's agony challenged the assumption of shared values and common transatlantic interests. It mocked Europe's ambitions for unity and greater presence on the global stage. And it raised a stark question about the continued seriousness of US military engagement in Europe. Something else happened during the three-and-a-half years of Bosnia's war: the Balkans were transformed in alliance calculations from a peripheral concern into *the* transatlantic security problem, at least if measured in terms of the time and attention demanded from allied leaders. There were of course many who argued, and continue to argue, that a marginal problem was thereby elevated to a primary one – distorting strategic priorities, especially in US foreign policy.

The consequences of disunity

Comparable in duration to the First World War, Yugoslavia's small, but fierce and prolonged conflicts similarly cut short what had been a moment of supreme optimism in European history. The crisis was familiar also in what set it off. The Serb national grievances that helped ignite war in 1914 were products of a very different, imperial age, of course, but they also foreshadowed a recurring twentieth century dilemma of self-determination in a multi-ethnic space. Some eight decades later, the minority Serbs in Kosovo, Croatia and Bosnia had some genuine grievances and plausible anxieties over their likely position should Yugoslavia come to an end. In this sense – of remembered and re-propagated ethno-national fears – the fighting was a reprise of the civil war, mainly between fascists and anti-fascists in which Serbs as well as Jews and Roma suffered disproportionately. The memories were exploited by nationalist demagogues – including Croat politicians but especially among the Serb leadership – who set out to dominate and then, failing this, to destroy Tito's Yugoslavia.

There was a third historical echo in the disorientation that the crisis inflicted upon Western democracies. Bosnia posed the archetypal international challenge of the 1990s: deciding whether, when and how to intervene in other people's wars. The problem is often analysed under the category of 'humanitarian interventions', but might better be labelled with the term 'asymmetric interventions'. To intervene in Bosnia raised dilemmas, identified by Lawrence Freedman, of countervailing asymmetries. A massive asymmetry of power in the West's favour seemed outweighed by a massive asymmetry of interests favouring the local protagonists. War for the West was becoming:

> ... *more a matter of choice than of necessity ... For the USA and its allies, this critical asymmetry of interests might be so sharp that they will see no purposes served by becoming involved and good reasons to keep clear: the intractability of the conflicts; their brutalising impact on all involved; the capacity of outsiders to make things worse rather than better; the ease of entry compared with that of exit.*

And yet, 'not all conflicts can be viewed with disinterest', as Freedman goes on to observe.[1] In such cases, the 'countervailing asymmetries' constituted for the West not a 'choice' but an extra burden: sooner or later, intervention had to come, but it seemed impossible to organise in a timely or effective manner. The 'choice', difficult enough for one power, became almost a parody of lowest-common-denominator decision-making when it had to be agreed among several allied powers. At least one of those powers always had a reason, or an alibi, for inaction.

In the case of Bosnia, the complexity of the crisis contributed to the moral and strategic paralysis of major Western powers and institutions until after the preferred solution was unequivocally forfeit.

Sarajevo did not fall, but much of Bosnian society was destroyed. Long after the Serbs' legitimate claims were dwarfed by the aggression committed in their name, Western policy was hobbled by its attempt at even-handedness. For the West's failures in Yugoslavia, there was plenty of blame to go around. But the very act of casting blame – notably between the United States and two of its principal European allies, Britain and France – made things worse. It constituted a subtext of such bitterness and intensity that it raised plausible doubts about the viability of transatlantic partnership, and institutionally weakened the United Nations.[2] More directly, transatlantic bickering had cruel consequences for Bosnia itself. To begin with, it prevented the West from mounting a show of force that might have persuaded the Serbs to respect UN resolutions. Until the summer of 1995, when *hubris* led it too far, the Serb leadership proved masterful at exploiting transatlantic disagreements about the use of force: last-minute concessions were finely calibrated to break the fragile Western consensus whenever robust military action looked imminent. The disagreements also undermined the most promising of the early peace proposals, unveiled in January 1993 by former US Secretary of State Cyrus Vance and former British Foreign Secretary David Owen.[3]

It would be wrong, therefore, to conclude that the cost of transatlantic divisions can be reckoned merely in abstract terms of lost NATO 'credibility'. The damage was far more specific and concrete. Because the allies were unable to agree among themselves on where and how to draw the line, they slid into effective acquiescence to the siege of Sarajevo and ethnic cleansing throughout Bosnia. Although the Bosnian Serbs suffered military reversal in the end, the *'Republika Srpska'* granted to them by Dayton was the nationally homogeneous product of three and a half years of terror, murder and mass expulsion. And while it cannot be proven, it is likely that this grim achievement in turn emboldened Belgrade, three years later, to imagine that a similar campaign of ethnic cleansing would be tolerated, and ultimately rewarded, in Kosovo. The costs of alliance disagreements therefore must be reckoned very high indeed.

A common confusion

To speak of 'transatlantic' divisions is to oversimplify. The disagreements were as much within as between the various NATO members. All allied powers were democracies possessed of easy moral outrage but limited willingness to commit lives, money and political capital in the Balkans. All allied powers were also subject to deep confusion about the legitimate and effective use of military force.

America: haunted by Vietnam

This shared confusion was particularly striking at the outset of Yugoslavia's unravelling. The administration of US President George Bush (the elder) had no strong views about how to handle the crisis distinct from the general European view.[4] Both Americans and Europeans were preoccupied with the impending disintegration of the Soviet federal state, and feared Yugoslavia's collapse above all for the precedent it might set. There was thus a general transatlantic agreement that federal unity should be preferred in both cases – at least until Germany started pressing in mid-1991 for diplomatic recognition of Croatia and Slovenia.

The Bush administration was also inclined for practical reasons to leave the problem in European hands. Bush had spent a great deal of political capital in the Gulf war and, notwithstanding an impressive military victory, was finding the domestic dividends to be meagre.[5] Moreover, European leaders appeared confident and eager to take on Bosnia by themselves.[6] All of this fell under the shadow of another episode in the recurring Franco-American quarrel, specifically about the future of NATO, but more broadly pitting the concept of an American-led, Atlantic 'community' against the Gaullist ambition of an independent, European superpower.[7]

The real transatlantic disagreement over the *substance* of the Bosnia crisis emerged during the Clinton administration. Bill Clinton's campaign to unseat Bush as president came at a time that American liberals were embracing Bosnia as a *cause célèbre*. By late 1992, the distinct horrors of the Bosnian war, of a different order than what had transpired in Croatia, were well known. The American and European press had powerfully conveyed the truth of ethnic cleansing – the use of terror, torture and mass murder to drive Muslims from their homes – and the reality that this was intrinsic to the Serb war aim of carving out ethnically homogenous territory. That summer, moreover, press and television reports emerged on concentration camps in central Bosnia, which resonated of the Nazi death camps. American inaction in the face of such revelations presented an obvious target for candidate Clinton.[8]

The idea of a significant military intervention fit the Vietnam generation of American liberals uncomfortably, however. Clinton himself – the first president since Roosevelt who had never worn a military uniform – was especially vulnerable to Pentagon resistance driven largely the senior US officer corps' personal memories of America's last great 'liberal' intervention, in Vietnam. The Chairman of the Joint Chiefs General Colin Powell, who had served in Vietnam, went public with his opposition to a military intervention in Bosnia a month before Clinton's election, drawing explicit comparisons to South-east Asia. It might not always be necessary to deploy American military forces in a posture of overwhelming military superiority, he argued, but any exceptions to this 'Powell Doctrine' should at least have clear military goals.[9] Like the jungles of South-east Asia, the mountains of Bosnia threatened to entangle American power and prestige – leaving American troops to bleed until some humiliating extrication. Vietnam was a potent political symbol. Colorado Senator Tim Wirth warned that 'the best liberal hope in a generation', could be dragged down by entanglement in Bosnia.[10] Historian Arthur Schlesinger Jr issued a similar warning – one that Clinton reportedly took to heart.[11] These warnings were underscored by the October 1993 debacle of 18 US soldiers killed in Mogadishu, cast by Clinton's many critics as a product of 'mission creep'.[12]

As applied to Bosnia, however, the Vietnam analogy was misleading on a number of counts that should have been – indeed, were – evident well before the summer of 1995. Bosnian Serb forces could hardly be compared to the Vietcong in their fanatic dedication. Long before the end of the war, there were indications that Bosnian Serb society was being hollowed out from within. Nearly every male of fighting age was enlisted or conscripted in military or police service, morale was low and drunkenness epidemic on the front lines. By contrast, after initial losses through the summer of 1992, it was the Bosnian government forces who proved surprisingly resilient, despite stark inferiority in weaponry. Belgrade, moreover, was certainly not a Hanoi prepared to endure a superpower's gruelling military punishment for a decade or more.

Europe: delusions of civilian grandeur

If America was confounded by one of its great failures, Europe was deluded by a recent success. In the early 1990s, it was perhaps inevitable that problems of European security would be viewed through the prism of the end of the Cold War. Europeans were generally happy to agree with William Pfaff's observation that 'it was the magnetism of the democracies' cooperative successes which irresistibly drew Eastern Europe and the Soviet Union towards western political values'.[13] For many Europeans, one of the overriding lessons was that 'soft power' was what they wielded most effectively and safely.[14] When it came to Yugoslavia, however, the Cold War successes fed some illusions. The EC 'troika' attempting to mediate an end to the Slovenian war, for example, seemed to assume that material incentives and the enlightening lure of European successes would persuade Yugoslav leaders to behave 'rationally'. As two perceptive journalists observed, international mediators sometimes 'behaved as though all they had to do was to persuade the belligerents of the folly of war. They failed to recognise that, in some circumstances, the resort to war was far from irrational'.[15]

Germany's push for EC recognition of the breakaway republics, Slovenia and Croatia, revealed a similar lack of realism. Germans had experienced the end of the Cold War above all through their own reunification, as a peaceful triumph of national self-determination. How, asked politicians in Bonn, could they presume to deny the aspirations of Croats and Slovenes who also sought to break free from Communist rule?[16] The difference, of course, was that the Soviet leadership under Mikhail Gorbachev chose to let the nations of Central and Eastern Europe go peacefully. Unlike Croatia with its anxious Serb minority, moreover, East Germany and Poland contained no Russian diaspora whose future would be clouded by the end of Soviet empire.[17]

The EC's diplomatic recognition of Croatia may have complicated peacemaking efforts – but in a long list of Western errors, this one should not be overemphasised. Germany's pressure certainly sowed suspicion among European partners, Britain in particular. Recognition undermined EC envoy Peter Carrington's quest for a comprehensive settlement for all of Yugoslavia, and removed the EU's greatest leverage for pressing Zagreb to respect Serb minority rights. However, the Carrington Plan – decisively rejected by Belgrade – was probably dead anyway. But Croatian independence did put Bosnia under strong pressure to follow suit; it was to avoid such pressures that Bosnian President Itzebegovic had publicly opposed recognition. Subsequently, Bosnia's own internationally supported referendum on independence precipitated – even if it did not, in a fundamental sense, cause – the Bosnian war.[18] Like the rest of the EU, Germany was unable or unwilling to deal with the consequences. Bonn's diplomatic tool kit contained only 'soft' or 'civilian' power. The same inadequacy characterised Western Europe as a whole – somewhat surprising when considered historically, since Britain and France are warrior nations with traditions of power projection and considerably less sensitivity to casualties than the US. Paris and London approached Bosnia, however, as a European problem which had to be dealt with in EU and United Nations frameworks. Policies formulated within these frameworks were influenced by the prevailing ethos of both institutions, under which soft power was naturally preferred over hard power.[19] Moreover, the European Community (as it was called until becoming the European 'Union' on 1 January 1993) was constitutionally organised in a way that reinforced the reliance on civilian power. Put simply, policy-making by intergovernmental consensus is ill-suited for the painful and controversial decisions required to wage war. In this light, the pattern of equivocation that characterised the European-dominated phase of diplomacy toward Bosnia should have come as no surprise.

Rhetoric and reality

Constitutional, historical and cultural factors on both sides of the Atlantic had the practical effect of making transatlantic policies converge around an ineffectual lowest common denominator. And yet the transatlantic debate about Bosnia – however detached from governments' actual policies – was acrimonious, with recognisable 'American' and 'European' voices. (Indeed, although European policies were not very effective, and although Germany in particular pursued policies that put it at odds with its European partners, the European *voice* was more distinct than usual, owing to a rare convergence of French and British perspectives *vis-à-vis* the US). The transatlantic acrimony centred on four emotional issues of principle:

- *Aggression*. Sarajevo's American supporters conceded that there had been crimes on all sides, but insisted that this could not be allowed to obscure what they regarded as a fundamental truth: that the recognised state of Bosnia was under brutal attack. For many European governments, matters were more complicated. If Bosnia was under attack, it was an attack from two sides and from within. From May 1993 until February 1994, Bosnian Croat forces, helped by Zagreb, conducted a brutal campaign of ethnic cleansing against Muslims in central Bosnia. The Serb and Croat projects were certainly abhorrent, but Europeans could not help noticing that war against the Bosnian government at times had the support of two out of three of Bosnia's ethnic groups. They questioned the realism – and therefore the humanity – of trying to defend a state whose existence seemed to be opposed by a majority of its inhabitants.

- *Ethnic cleansing*. The Bosnian war had started in April 1992, with Serb-Yugoslav regular and irregular troops laying siege to Sarajevo and conducting campaigns of murder, torture, rape and expulsion against Muslim and Croat communities in eastern and northern Bosnia. Some serious observers of what was happening in Bosnia applied the word 'genocide'.[20] The label was problematic, for although the definition contained in the United Nations' 1948 Genocide Convention was arguably broad enough to encompass Bosnia's ethnic cleansing, such programmes of mass extermination as against the Jews in the Second World War, or in Rwanda in 1994, were clearly crimes of a different order.[21] Even if 'civilians were targeted because of their ethnicity', there was an arguable case that the war in Bosnia was still a 'traditional war over territory'.[22] Others noted that ethnic cleansing was an old tradition in the region. But these complications did not negate the reality that a war directed mainly against civilians, on account of their ethnicity, raised special problems and, arguably, obligations for the Western powers. In 2001, moreover, in a carefully reasoned judgement against Bosnian Serb General Radislav Krstic, Hague-tribunal judges confirmed that – in at least the case of the Srebrenica massacre – 'genocide' was indeed planned and implemented.[23]

- *The UN arms embargo.* The embargo applied to all the warring former Yugoslav republics, including Bosnia. The Americans argued that the blanket arms embargo had the effect of denying a recognised member of the United Nations the means to defend itself. Europeans pointed out that the United States was a veto-wielding member of the Security Council that had imposed the embargo in the first place, and they wondered how Washington could justify having one policy in the UN Security Council, and another policy on the ground of encouraging the flow of arms to Muslim forces.

- *The use of force.* Some Americans argued – until it became a refrain – that in the face of determined aggression, diplomacy not backed by force was quickly revealed as empty posturing. The Europeans, including the UK and French governments, had some good and bad reasons to be reluctant to use force, although their reluctance waned over the course of 1994 and 1995. What did not change, however, was their angry conviction that the Americans were the emptiest posturers of all: Washington talked about force a great deal, but was not willing to apply it, except occasionally from the air.

These four issues confounded and divided the alliance, frequently along transatlantic lines. But again, the contending transatlantic voices were hardly uniform: inside every NATO power there was indecision, inconsistency and a cacophony of arguments. It might be more accurate to speak of the transatlantic divide in terms of prevailing 'attitudes'. Indeed, what made the alliance divisions particularly debilitating was that, although each side had distinctive attitudes, neither side was ready to implement policies that coherently reflected those attitudes. Washington, for example, purported to support the Sarajevo government; yet was hardly ready to organise the large troop presence that would have been necessary to defend and incubate a Bosnian state, or even to repudiate fully the UN arms embargo and openly supply weapons to the Muslims. On the other side, many European officials expressed 'realistic' scepticism about the viability of a multi-ethnic Bosnian state. Yet, no European government was prepared to act on this supposed realism by putting forward and implementing a plan for population transfers and three-way partition.

Bosnian statehood

Over the course of the war, all the Western powers moved towards a position of more direct intervention on the side of the Sarajevo government and the Muslims, whom public opinion on both sides of the Atlantic overwhelmingly supported.[24] Washington, however, was consistently more ready to support the Sarajevo government – at least rhetorically. There were many reasons for these differences. It is probably true that figures such as French President François Mitterrand had difficulty confronting the leaders of a nation that had joined with the Anglo-French allies in two world wars. Close observers of the UN Protection Force (UNPROFOR) alleged that some of its top officers found Bosnian Serb commanders more professional and more congenial than their Muslim counterparts.[25] Moreover, there was considerable distrust of the Muslims' claims to represent the cause of ethnic tolerance.[26] Distrust was intensified by the perception – no doubt justified – that the Muslims would do almost anything to draw UNPROFOR into the fighting.[27]

Matters were further clouded by Croatia's role. As a practical matter, the debate about supporting Sarajevo was a debate about NATO military action against Bosnian Serb forces. But the Serbs were not the only ones trying to dismember Bosnia. Tudjman secretly met Milosevic in 1991 to discuss dividing Bosnia and Herzegovina between Belgrade and Zagreb.[28] He never wavered in his political and military support for the extreme nationalists among Bosnian Croats, nor in his open contempt for the Muslims.[29] To those who discussed matters with both men, it seemed obvious that Tudjman was a more fanatical nationalist that the opportunistic Milosevic.[30] Yet Tudjman was able to pursue a more opportunistic policy towards Bosnia, sometimes joining forces with the Muslims, and at other times fighting them, while much of the time enjoying a tacit strategic partnership with the United States. That partnership caused consternation among some West European officials and analysts, who felt that it robbed US policy of moral legitimacy.

More broadly, West Europeans found it difficult to find heroes and take sides in a fratricidal and historically complicated crisis. With more limited historical involvement, and no troops on the ground, Washington could afford to take a simpler view and support Sarajevo without reservation. And, in truth, this was arguably one of those times when the less nuanced American moral vocabulary served it better than the Europeans' more complex and tragic sense of history. Some simplifying was necessary to make coherent policy in a confused crisis. Support for Sarajevo was consistent, moreover, with the logic of European policies toward Yugoslavia since 1990. Peter Carrington, in his capacity as the first EC peace envoy, had produced a framework for conceding the dissolution of Yugoslavia only as part of a comprehensive agreement, under which minority rights would enjoy concrete protections. Robert Badinter's EC Arbitration Commission sensibly used some of the same principles in setting up a process to determine which individual Yugoslav republics met the criteria for European Community recognition. Out of this process came the decision by both the EC and United States to recognise Bosnia and Herzegovina's independence. Notwithstanding Bosnian Serb opposition to and many Bosnian Croats' discomfort with the idea of a Bosnian state, once Sarajevo conducted the independence referendum that the EU had urged it to conduct and won international recognition of Bosnian statehood, it only confused matters to act as though the Sarajevo government's involvement in a civil war diminished its legitimacy.[31] The Bosnian war was a civil war, to be sure; but at the same time it was a war of aggression, planned and carried out by the Serb leadership in Belgrade and Pale and, from 1993, by Croats in Herzegovina and Zagreb. The international dimension of the war was also clear: it was an attack against Bosnia, by Serbia in the first instance, and later by Croatia.

The debate about the 'authenticity' of Bosnia as an historical entity within the Austro-Hungarian or Ottoman empires tended to obscure a more urgent issue: even if an autonomous Bosnia was something new under the sun, its existence as a state was the only plausible hope to stave off disaster once the shelter of a Yugoslav federation had cracked apart. Unlike Bosnian Serbs and Croats, Bosnian Muslims had no mother state to adhere to, and the idea of herding them into a residual Muslim territory – left over after Serb and Croat land-grabs – was morally dubious and politically and strategically infeasible. The Itzetbegovic government, though it succumbed sometimes to the trappings of 'Bosniac' nationalism, had a plausible claim to have offered a state in which all three ethnic groups could live (and enjoyed support in this project from a modest but significant number of moderate Croats and Serbs). The viability of this offered state was questionable, but the alternatives were worse. In this regard, Bosnia was in the same class as Macedonia, another Yugoslav republic whose ethnic resentments were just as deep and whose viability as a state was also suspect. Indeed, a lack of confidence in their own statehood, which Macedonia and Bosnia shared from the outset, had united their presidents in a last-ditch effort to save some sort of Yugoslav federation or confederation. When that effort failed, Americans and Europeans had no difficulty in agreeing that Macedonian independence and state survival were critical, the only effective shelter against ethnic conflict and even general war in the south Balkans.

America's case against Europe

Americans were perplexed that many among their European allies seemed to find it more difficult to reach the same conclusion about Bosnia. In practice, Bosnia's collapse into war perhaps made such support more difficult, but also more important. No fair-minded partisan of the Sarajevo government would deny that some atrocities were committed by Muslims. And many Croats were certainly implicated in terrible crimes. But the largest share of such acts – the original attacks on both Croatia and Bosnia and the most open and sustained defiance of UN resolutions – came from the Serb side.[32] Here the common generalisation about American naïveté, of a tendency to see things in shades of black and white, can be turned on its head. The more simplistic moralism is to insist that a state or society be perfectly democratic and morally unblemished before it deserves being defended against attack.

Arming the Muslims

Despite its campaign rhetoric, the Clinton administration was not ready to overrule Pentagon opposition to a direct intervention. It fell back on the alternative of 'lift and strike' – i.e., a plan to lift the arms embargo against the Sarajevo government and support its freshly armed fighters from the air. In fact, the United States dropped its official advocacy of 'lift and strike' after a May 1993 European tour by US Secretary of State Warren Christopher encountered solid opposition in Paris and London, and after President Clinton started to express qualms about even that degree of American engagement.[33] But it remained a popular concept in American politics, uniting elements of left and right. Many argued that, since 'lift and strike' was the most the US and Europe could do under prevailing political conditions, it was better than nothing.[34]

For the French and British, it was a source of constant irritation that Washington, while apparently eager to join the war from the relative safety of the air, refused to risk its own ground troops. This complaint, while understandable, does not address the central point of the Americans' argument: that it was wrong to deprive a sovereign government under attack of the means to defend itself. Many Americans felt that the international arms embargo put the entire United Nations effectively on the side of the Serbs, who had enough heavy weaponry to continue the war for years. This US perception reflected an historical rule of thumb: blanket arms embargoes usually penalise the victims of aggression, given that the aggressor – almost by definition – is adequately armed already.[35]

With Congress pressing to lift the arms embargo unilaterally, if necessary, the US might well have found itself in the position of openly violating a Security Council resolution and outraging its allies.[36] In the event, the Clinton administration found an opportunity for a compromise when Croatian President Tudjman asked Peter Galbraith, the US ambassador in Zagreb, what attitude Washington might take towards the secret delivery of weapons through Croatia to Bosnia. On instructions from Washington, Galbraith replied that he had 'no instructions' – an implicit green light. Galbraith himself argues that the subsequent flow of arms – including controversial deliveries from Iran – probably prevented the fall of Sarajevo. 'It was a close thing'.[37]

The use of force

The debate about 'lift and strike' tapped into one of the deepest sources of American anger at European allies. The issue went beyond the question of likely risk to UNPROFOR troops, to a more fundamental transatlantic divide over relative values of war and peace. Some Americans accused the Europeans of wanting peace at almost any price. There may have been some truth in this criticism, although it was also true that troops operating under a UN peacekeeping mandate, in coordination with a UN Secretariat following a doctrine of 'impartiality', faced genuine dilemmas. The UN's humanitarian response to the war implied a 'humanitarian' definition of the crisis, and the transition to a political–military alignment with one of the warring parties was inevitably going to be awkward.

To some extent, a peacekeeping mandate implied a commitment to the status quo, since changing it would mean more war. Pale (the ski village that Bosnian Serbs proclaimed as their capital) was not terribly dissatisfied with the status quo either, since by mid-1992 its soldiers had already conquered and cleansed more than two-thirds of the country. It was rather the Bosnian government in Sarajevo that was most unhappy and, therefore, increasingly the party of continued war. To further complicate matters, French and British UNPROFOR commanders answered to two masters: the United Nations Secretariat and their own respective national governments. Both sources of authority were reluctant to use force, and their reluctance was mutually reinforcing. UN officials complained that their organisation had become a scapegoat for key Security Council members who were themselves unwilling to confront the Serbs, and who handed down 'impractical, unenforceable, crucially ambiguous mandates'.[38] The complaint was accurate enough, but it also constituted a convenient alibi: for the UN had its own institutional philosophy, influence and responsibility, as acknowledged in a 1999 UN report – a stunning institutional *mea culpa* – from Secretary-General Kofi Annan. While unsparing in its criticism of other international players, the report also dissects the role of the Secretariat itself at the centre of an international response that Serb leaders quickly learned how to paralyse. It examines the fall of Srebrenica, and the Serb massacre of some 7,000 unarmed men and boys there, as the most grievous consequence of a host of UN policy errors: a ludicrous 'dual-key' command arrangement for authorising the use of force (which usually meant blocking it); a prism of 'moral equivalency' through which 'the conflict ... was viewed by too many for too long'; and a 'failure to fully comprehend' that 'civilian inhabitants of the enclaves were not the incidental victims of the [Serb] attackers; their death or removal was the very purpose of the attacks upon them'.

> *In the end, these Bosnian Serb war aims were ultimately repulsed on the battlefield, and not at the negotiating table. Yet, the Secretariat had convinced itself early on that the*

broader use of force by the international community was beyond our mandate and anyway undesirable. A report of the Secretary-General to the Security Council spoke against a 'culture of death', arguing that peace should be pursued only through non-military methods ...The cardinal lesson of Srebrenica is that a deliberate and systematic attempt to terrorise, expel or murder an entire people must be met decisively with all necessary means. In the Balkans, in this decade, this lesson has had to be learned not once, but twice. In both instances, in Bosnia and in Kosovo, the international community tried to reach a negotiated settlement with an unscrupulous and murderous regime. In both instances it required the use of force to bring a halt to the planned and systematic killing and expulsion of civilians.[39]

'Pacifist' UN bureaucrats, along with European 'appeasers', are the kinds of stereotypes easily thrown about in the American political discourse. Regarding Bosnia, they were thrown about in a manner that seemed to assume that the United States – the most powerful member of the Security Council, not to mention NATO – had only limited influence over the course of Western policy. Yet the UN itself came to acknowledge that this critique of the reluctance to use of force, however selectively focused, was also valid.

Europe's case against America

To this general charge of appeasement, David Owen gave the most succinct European response in early 1993. 'Munich,' he said, 'was last year' – meaning that the time to save Bosnia had been the spring of 1992, when there was still a Bosnia to be defended.[40] The years 1990–92 made up a period of considerable plasticity in the crisis: if the Western allies had credibly threatened and/or used force early enough – at the time of the shelling of Dubrovnik and Vukovar would have been an obvious early opportunity – Serbs might have reflected more soberly on the likelihood of their ultimate defeat. NATO SACEUR John Galvin produced a plan for repelling the attack on Dubrovnik in 1991, and the then US Ambassador to Belgrade Warren Zimmermann would argue, in retrospect, that it should have been used.[41] But capitals on both sides of the Atlantic – the Bush administration even more clearly than the Europeans –

made clear their unwillingness to contemplate intervening with military force. For more than two years, the Clinton administration was no more willing.

From a European point of view, morality and realism went together. The first moral obligation of the outside powers was to give the Sarajevo government a true picture of what it could reasonably expect. Europeans were indignant at what they considered a characteristically American gap between words and deeds, between rhetoric and commitment.[42] Through 'lift and strike', Washington wanted to intensify the war; this was literally irresponsible, since it would be non-American UNPROFOR troops who would suffer the consequences of an intensified war. Through its rhetoric, Washington discouraged Sarajevo from settling for an imperfect peace, but the US was never willing to exert the military muscle that would have been necessary to impose any deal better than Vance-Owen. To be sure, neither were the Europeans.

Sabotaging Europe's peace plan?

The Vance-Owen Peace Plan was just one of a series of eight UN, European and 'Contact Group' proposals for ending the war in Bosnia.[43] It shared many of the characteristics of those that came before and after. There are two reasons for concentrating so much attention on it. Firstly, it was the last of the plans to be based on a scheme of decentralised cantonisation, rather than clear territorial division. Secondly, although one of its authors was a former US Secretary of State, it was 'Europe's plan' insofar as the major European governments embraced it unreservedly, while Washington refused to commit itself.

The plan would have recast Bosnia and Herzegovina as a decentralised state of three constituent peoples, ten provinces or cantons, with a special status for Sarajevo and a loose central government. Its canton arrangement was no doubt unwieldy. And many observers have blamed the presumption that each canton would be dominated by one of the three ethnic groups for at least some of the ethnic cleansing between the Croats and the Muslims that intensified after the plan was unveiled.[44] However, the American charge that it rewarded ethnic cleansing was rather hard for Europeans to swallow, especially in retrospect, for each subsequent peace plan went a further step in recognising Bosnia's ethnic separation. Its authors, certainly, but also many dispassionate observers felt that Vance-Owen represented the last and best chance to halt this disintegration.[45]

The continuing bitterness of European diplomats and leaders at the US criticisms has contributed, perhaps, to some myths. Sarajevo did eventually accept the Vance-Owen Peace Plan, while the Bosnian Serbs rejected it. Thus it is difficult to sustain the argument that lack of US support constituted the decisive element that doomed the Vance-Owen diplomacy. It is probably true, however, that obtaining Pale's agreement would have required immediate and unflinching American support – with a strong message that the plan would be imposed on any party that refused to sign. Owen, to his credit, had a consistent view and a consistent strategy: sign up the Muslims and Croats, then isolate the Bosnian Serbs (which also meant isolating Pale from Belgrade, something that was accomplished rather well), and finally impose Vance-Owen, with military force if necessary.[46] The Americans, by contrast, were anything but consistent. In the first month of 1993, the unveiling of the Vance-Owen Peace Plan inspired overwhelmingly negative commentary in the American press, the general line of which was that the plan would reward ethnic cleansing.[47] The Clinton administration, arriving in office the same month, let it be known that it was uneasy about and certainly uncommitted to the plan. It blocked a strong UN Security Council endorsement, and refused to pressure the Izetbegovic government to sign (the Bosnian Croats had signed almost immediately).

No one can prove, counterfactually, that with strong American support Vance-Owen would have succeeded. One can only observe that such support was not given.[48]

American inconsistency

Europeans became especially indignant as they started to comprehend the logic of American diplomacy after the plan's demise. Vance-Owen, according to that logic, had been infeasible because it did not concede *enough* to the Serb side.[49] As Owen himself interpreted it, Washington simply had no stomach for US troops (promised as part of an implementation force) having to patrol so many borders on such a patchwork of cantons – especially if they had to 'confront Bosnian Serb forces who were not ready to withdraw'.[50] On the other hand, Dayton (and to a lesser extent, the

Contact Group plans leading up to Dayton) were based on a simpler and, arguably, more realistic map. Dayton may have been more negotiable precisely because it granted Pale the essential ideological victory of an autonomous *Republika Srpska*, and because subsequent US diplomacy forged a working Croat–Muslim alliance that later translated into a single federation to face the Serb entity. The map of Dayton was 'cleaner' in this sense; achieving it, however, required further ethnic cleansing. And therein lay the fundamental American inconsistency. Until late 1995, the US government refused to contemplate imposing any settlement, either by exerting pressure on the Muslims or using military force against the Serbs. It continually fed the hopes of the Bosnian government that the United States would actually do something to defend those values that it kept proclaiming.[51] It refused to consider deploying ground troops – a refusal that David Owen has accurately called the 'exposed jugular of American policy'.[52]

Lessons learned?

The US strategic approach proved effective in the end. But it was effective in strictly limited terms. Relying, as it did, on Bosnian government and especially Croat forces to turn the tide, the best it could achieve was to carve out a more decently minimal space for the besieged Muslims in a dismembered Bosnia and Herzegovina. This was no small achievement, though it certainly fell short of the standards that Washington was proclaiming in early 1993. And it took two more years and many thousands more deaths to get to it.

It is proper to speak of an American 'strategic approach', rather than a 'strategy', because the critical events of summer 1995 were not planned in Washington or anywhere else. What the United States really brought to the search for a solution was a brand of 'strategic opportunism'. The most consciously planned and, at the time, most underrated, strategic element was the 1994 Washington Agreement between Muslims and Croats, which ended their own civil war and laid the basis for a reconstituted anti-Serb alliance. Following upon that agreement came a series of American opportunities:

- to encourage an arms flow via Zagreb to Bosnia (in the face of the UN embargo);
- to encourage a Croat offensive recapturing the Krajina;

- to collaborate with Milosevic in isolating the Pale leadership;
- to push NATO into a serious bombing campaign after Srebrenica, the subsequent London Conference and another 'market-place massacre' in Sarajevo; and
- to synchronise the Holbrooke diplomacy of September 1995 with both the NATO bombing and the Croat–Muslim offensive.

If the US was better placed to seize these opportunities, it was partly because of its preponderant power and prestige, but also because its default 'attitudes' were more appropriate to the crisis. These included using force and taking sides. The UN template of 'impartiality' was not just morally problematic, but also the source of strategic incoherence. A settlement proved possible only after the Croat–Muslim side gained the offensive on the ground; and after Serb *hubris* (the seizure of UNPROFOR hostages and the massacres of Srebrenica) finally provoked NATO into joining the war as an ally, in effect, of the Sarajevo government.

In some cases, taking sides meant choosing a lesser evil. In April and May 1995, Zagreb launched a military operation to recover control of Western Slavonia. Then, on 4 August, the Croatian army launched *Operation Storm* to retake the Serb-held Krajina. There was scant Serb resistance, and no support from Belgrade. Some 180,000 Serbs fled, abandoning what were – in many cases – centuries-old Serb communities. The exodus was encouraged by a Croat campaign of ethnic cleansing.[53] *Operation Storm* was a critical element of the broad Croat–Muslim sweep through west-central Bosnia that turned the tide of war and forced Pale to settle for the Dayton peace. Critics have judged harshly what they regard as Washington's complicity in *Operation Storm* and, by extension, the ethnic cleansing that followed. Yet, this criticism leaves unanswered the question of how Serb forces were going to be defeated if not through a combined Croat–Muslim offensive that included Zagreb's recapture of the Krajina. US officials concede that they registered no serious objections when Zagreb informed them of plans for *Operation Storm* and expected that most Serbs would flee. Yet assessing this American green light – for the offensive, not the cleansing – requires some appreciation of its context. Following the mass slaughter at Srebrenica and the fall of Zepa, Bosnian Serb General Ratko Mladic's forces responded to Croat–Muslim successes in central

Bosnia by closing in on the Muslim-held Bihac pocket. Bihac was encircled by Serb troops in Krajina as well as in Bosnia. The best way to relieve Bihac was to attack Krajina. And after the killings in Srebrenica, according to Galbraith, Washington saw the threat to Bihac's Muslims in an alarming new light: 'By Srebrenica rules, many thousands [of men and older boys] would have been killed ... we decided not to object [to *Operation Storm*] based on this moral calculation'.[54]

It is difficult to quarrel with this calculation, or with the broader strategic judgement that a Croat–Muslim ground offensive through central Bosnia was to be encouraged as the only politically realistic means to defeat Serb forces and end the war. Among the lessons learned, therefore, is that American 'strategic opportunism' was the best of the alliance policies on offer. In crediting Washington, however, one cannot absolve the US of its share of the blame for more than three years of passivity. The United States was consistently less willing than the British or French to sacrifice its own soldiers to save Muslim lives. The hollowness at the heart of the UN 'safe areas' policy, of which Srebrenica stands as the grimmest emblem, was an American failing as much as a UN or European abdication.

If Washington shares much of the blame, its European allies deserve some of the credit for the renewed energy of Western policy after Srebrenica. In some measure, it was the anger of the new French President Jacques Chirac – infuriated by the Serb taking of French hostages as well as shamed by the fall of Srebrenica – that helped spur US President Bill Clinton into more resolute action.[55] The UNPROFOR Commander, British General Rupert Smith, helped engineer an important change in military thinking about the crisis, finally proving eager to implement a harder and 'disproportionate' response to Serb violations of UN resolutions and common decency. The deployment by London and Paris of a Rapid Reaction Force with heavy artillery to pound Serb positions around Sarajevo was, in military terms, as important as NATO's aerial bombardment.

These stipulations provide a truer, more balanced assessment of responsibilities, but they are also important for the insights they offer into the nature of alliance decision-making, and the obstacles to action. In practice, overcoming paralysis in the face of a war that threatened values, but not – directly – core security, required a substantial convergence of outrage and determination among the key Western allies. A final conclusion, therefore, is perhaps the most frustrating for analysts and planners. Mutual paralysis – even in the face of great evil – is in the nature of a democratic alliance. This suggests that crises must truly 'ripen' before outside powers can come together to address them. Once they have ripened, however, much of the opportunity for an effective intervention will have been lost. This frustrating reality would be demonstrated again, three years later, in Kosovo.

Chapter 2

Dayton and the American Problem

From 1995 through 1999, NATO allies tried to forge a common approach to the post-Dayton Balkans. They achieved a measure of success. Shared remorse at having failed for so long to confront the attacks on Bosnia made NATO more ready to use force in Kosovo. The same collective hangover also encouraged the NATO allies to agree, implicitly at least, on two conclusions concerning the structure of alliance relations.

Firstly, the alliance itself had been threatened by the war in Bosnia. In future Balkan crises it would be necessary to defuse that threat. For the Europeans, and particularly the French, this meant recognising that it was a costly mistake to make Balkans policy a vehicle for unrealistic (or at least premature) European projects, or for Gaullist resentment of US dominance. Conversely, on the US side there was a recognition that *Schadenfreude* about European inadequacies was misplaced, for Europe's failures in the Balkans rebounded to damage American credibility. Washington could not protect that credibility by maintaining that the US had no vital interests in the region.

The second conclusion was that US engagement was critical. Americans and Europeans interpreted this lesson somewhat differently, however. The US view, in Holbrooke's words, was that 'Unless the United States is prepared to put its political and military muscle behind the quest for solutions to European instability, nothing really gets done'.[1] The European interpretation was more complicated: only a significant US military involvement, even US 'leadership', could protect the Europeans from another traumatic experience in which they took responsibility for conflict resolution while the US enjoyed the power and the licence to criticise and even undermine European efforts.

Uncertainties of US engagement

Yet if US engagement was vital to managing Balkans security, there was also an enduring American problem. Its symptoms were fear of 'mission creep', fixation on 'exit strategy', a near 'zero-tolerance' for casualties and, more generally, uncertain commitment. Europeans may have suffered from some or all of these disabilities as well. However, in the US case they were magnified – partly for cultural reasons, but mainly for geopolitical ones. Whereas European interests in Balkan stability were obvious, direct and enduring, American interests were indirect and subject to constant debate about their relative importance in a context of US global responsibilities.

American ambivalence about European engagements is almost a cliché, despite the US role in two world wars, its Cold War leadership and its very risky nuclear guarantee in NATO. It is nonetheless an historical reality. Throughout the twentieth century, a genuine – if limited – isolationist impulse was driven mainly by political and cultural currents that ranged from ambivalence to open hostility towards alliances with the major European powers. Advocates of a strong US engagement usually carried the day, but not before a debate that injected some damaging uncertainty into the alliance system. Moreover, this vigorous Atlanticism did not always prevail: its emblematic failure was of President Woodrow Wilson's attempt to secure American participation in the League of Nations.

Then, as now, the uncertainties of US engagement posed a problem for European allies. Harold Nicolson, with the British delegation to the 1919 peace conference, observed first-hand this distinctively American combination of lofty ideals, immense power and inconstant application:

> *Mr. Wilson had not invented any new political philosophy, or discovered any doctrine which had not been dreamed of, and appreciated, for many hundred years. The one thing that rendered Wilsonism so passionately interesting at the moment was the fact that this centennial dream was*

suddenly backed by the overwhelming resources of the strongest Power in the world.[2]

Wilsonian ideals raised immense expectations in inter-war Europe and at home in the United States. The disappointment was mutual. On the European side, the inability to count on American armed support reinforced the fearful and vindictive application of the Versailles Treaty. Such enduring enmity in turn helped convince many Americans that the quarrels in Europe were quarrels between various kinds of rogues.

For half a century after Pearl Harbor, the anti-European element at the heart of classic 'isolationism' became dormant, even if it did not entirely vanish. While there was no lack of debate and controversy in American politics about how to wage the Cold War, the vital US interest in European security was taken more or less for granted. Ambivalence resurfaced in 1992, with the war in Yugoslavia. America had no 'dog in that fight' – such was then Secretary of State James Baker's colourful formulation of the Bush administration's strategic assessment. The Clinton administration may have challenged this conclusion rhetorically, but tended in practice to fall back on the same assessment.[3]

By summer 1995, the miscalculation at the heart of these assessments had become obvious.[4] In effect, Washington was saying that so long as it made clear that there was no possibility of US intervention, no American credibility would be staked, or lost. This idea contained the implausible assumption that the United States could stand passive in the face of a brutal, constantly televised war in territory that lay between Athens and Vienna – and that such passivity would not affect its stature or its leadership of NATO. In fact, America's eventual engagement was pre-programmed into its alliance relationships; the only question was whether it would engage successfully, or be sucked into a disaster. In NATO's Operations Plan (OPLAN) 40104, the United States had committed an eventual 20,000 troops to help extract UNPROFOR peacekeepers.[5] And a decision by the key UNPROFOR countries to withdraw was looking increasingly likely in the spring of 1995. The American promise to help them leave was hardly a whimsical or even optional commitment: anything less would certainly have done further damage to US claims to leadership. Yet, to have fulfilled the promise would have also constituted a political and moral debacle. There were plausible predictions of wailing women and children sitting down to block the retreat of UNPROFOR vehicles – a drama that would have been broadcast into American homes. The shift in military fortunes and diplomacy in the late summer and fall of 1995 meant that US troops could be sent to preside over peace, rather than a Western retreat.

Dayton did not, however, dispel powerful doubts in the United States about the wisdom of an open-ended commitment in the Balkans. Congress, with a newly elected Republican majority contemptuous of President Clinton's leadership, was overwhelming hostile to a lengthy deployment of US peacekeeping troops. Such hostility was encouraged by a Pentagon leadership still loath to commit its troops to another project of 'nation building'. In Washington and New York, within the tightly knit community of non-governmental foreign-policy analysts, doubts about the Bosnia engagement provided the occasion for a broader debate about the terms of the transatlantic security bargain. Scepticism was especially strong on the centre-right. Henry Kissinger, for example, argued that the Bosnian peace agreement made, in effect, another false Wilsonian promise that did not square with true US interests.[6] Others saw NATO itself as increasingly irrelevant to US strategic interests – unless it could be transformed in a 'grand bargain' by which the Europeans joined together more assertively to combat such global problems as terrorism and weapons of mass destruction in the hands of Saddam Hussein.[7] During the Persian Gulf crisis of winter 1997–98, for example, US congressmen could be hear to question why America should 'help the Europeans in Bosnia if the French don't help us in Iraq?'.[8]

A standard reaction to such scepticism was an appeal to history, in which Dayton represented the third time in a century that the United States returned to Europe to save Europe from itself. It did so, in this appeal, because Europe's wars threatened vital American interests. Richard Holbrooke, interviewed four months after Dayton, commented that 'it took some time to realize that we are still part of the balance of power in Europe'.[9] But where was the significant threat to that balance, comparable to Stalin, Hitler or Wilhelmine Germany? Those who were sceptical of an American vocation to grapple with Europe's second-tier ethnic conflicts could argue, as Ronald Steel did, that:

The United States is not a European nation, any more than it is an Asian nation. It is an Atlantic power, and a Pacific one, with interests in both continents. During the Cold War, as in the two other European wars of this century, that interest lay in preventing any single nation – and particularly a hostile, totalitarian one – from gaining control of the continent. That remains an American interest; but that is not the problem confronting Europe today.[10]

Listening to this debate, European leaders had two kinds of responses. On the one hand, they had new motivation to reduce their security dependence on the United States. NATO summit and ministerial meetings in 1994 and 1996 took a step in this direction, at least on paper. The Combined Joint Task Force (CJTF) concept, an agreement that 'coalitions of the willing' could draw on NATO assets to perform missions in which the United States might not be directly involved, constituted an implicit recognition from both sides of the Atlantic that European members of NATO might have to address security interests – or even moral obligations – that the United States would not directly share. More practical steps came after the election of Britain's Labour government under Tony Blair, who reversed long-standing British policy by embracing, together with French President Jacques Chirac, the goal of autonomous European defence capabilities.[11]

The other, and more immediate, European response seemed to contradict these aspirations. As the Dayton Implementation Force (IFOR) was being organised, Europeans insisted that they would not maintain ground troops in Bosnia without US participation. Indeed, with their nerves still jarred by the UNPROFOR experience, European officials warned Washington that the moment American troops left, theirs would leave too. Their refrain, 'in together, out together', was explained in early 1996 by a high-ranking official in the German Foreign Ministry:

The joint presence of us all, especially the United States, is a major factor for cohesion … When we had Franco-British forces on the ground, but no US and no German, it was a recipe for tension. If cohesion is needed for long-term implementation of Dayton, it is important to stay together

> *militarily … Having US air support is not the same. You*
> *can see it in the way we cooperate now as opposed to a year*
> *ago, when we had a very severe rift. Then there was French*
> *and British resistance [to using military force]. German*
> *fundamentalists saying 'punish the Serbs' – but no troops.*
> *The US knew better on everything. The Russians were*
> *always saying 'nyet'.*[12]

In less polite terms, Paris, London and other European capitals were determined never again to deploy ground troops in Bosnia while Washington, in their view, indulged a rhetorical idealism, with no American lives at risk, and was careless about working at cross purposes with what the Europeans were trying to accomplish.

Peace enforcement, 1995–2001

Dayton's ambiguities reflected both the mixed fortunes of the war and the confusion of the international response. Dayton Bosnia created two separate entities – including a *'Republika Srpska'* utterly 'cleansed' of Muslims and Croats. Most state powers devolved to the entities, which also retained their own armed forces. This extreme degree of devolution is one of several reasons that some close observers argue that the key element ending the war was not so much the NATO bombing as the concessions to Serb war aims.[13] In late 1996, Nikola Koljevic, then vice-president of *Republika Srpska*, commented: 'I could not believe it at first that NATO was willing to send 60,000 troops to separate us from the Muslims. After all, that's what we fought for for three years'.[14] Such sentiments help to explain why IFOR had little difficulty implementing the military aspects of the agreement: the separation of opposing forces and collection of most of their heavy weapons.[15]

The point here is not to condemn Dayton for being a compromise, which peace agreements generally are. Moreover, there is nothing inherently illegitimate about a radical devolution of authority to a state's constituent entities. What critics have described as a central government 'designed to be non-functional', might more generously be described as a consensus-based system to protect the 'vital interests' of Bosnia's three constituent nationalities.[16] Such mechanisms of ethnic protection, after all, were embedded in the old Yugoslav system. Rather, the dilemma of Dayton is that while its divisive aspects reflected the concrete results of the war, its *unifying* elements were merely paper commitments requiring either the good faith of the recently warring parties to honour them, or an outside party determined to enforce them.

Enforcement from the outside required a security force ready to take on the task. IFOR resisted, for a variety of reasons anchored in the Pentagon's long-standing unease about Bosnia. In the run-up to the Dayton peace talks, important interagency negotiations within the US government had pitted the military establishment against Holbrooke's team at the State Department. The Pentagon position was that IFOR's mandate should be limited to separating the combatants and controlling cease-fire lines. Holbrooke wanted a far more intrusive mandate to include such difficult tasks as backing up police security, escorting returning refugees across inter-entity lines (the new internal borders), securing general freedom of movement, overseeing elections and arresting war criminals. Holbrooke was never likely to win such arguments. Polls showed some 70% of the US public opposed sending troops to Bosnia.[17] Congressional hostility – and Congress' 'umbilical connection' to the Pentagon, as one White House official has put it – helped determine the outcome.

This Pentagon victory was significant. For a critical 18 months after Dayton, it is fair to say that none of the agreement's unifying provisions was substantially implemented. The formation of common institutions was blocked mainly from the Serb side; once established, they functioned sporadically if at all. Freedom of movement between entities was, for much of this time, non-existent; illegal roadblocks dotted the landscape, and the ethnic identification provided by 'Federation' or '*Republika Srpska*' licence plates rendered any Muslim or Croat so foolhardy as to cross into Serb territory highly vulnerable. Divided media, under the firm control of three nationalist leaderships, continued to spew out hate propaganda. The malign power of that propaganda was quickly felt. A first critical benchmark for a reunified Bosnia came in early 1996, when the Sarajevo suburbs of Ilidza and Grbavica were to be turned over by the Serbs to Federation control. Whether the Serbs living there would remain under a Sarajevo government was seen as a first test of the Dayton project. The failure was dramatic.

For weeks before the handover, Pale harangued the Serbs to flee. Bosnian Serb police and thug accomplices went door to door to underscore the message, and then put both suburbs to torch. These fires, raging for days under the noses of heavily armed NATO troops, underscored for all parties concerned where IFOR's commanders defined the limits of their mandate and role. They resisted being drawn into policing.[18] Nor was there any impartial police force to provide security for all Bosnians. Although the Dayton agreement mandated an 'International Police Task Force' (IPTF) of police officers seconded from various sponsoring powers, in practice the IPTF was poorly funded, understaffed and unarmed. Its mandate was limited to observation and training of Bosnia's existing ethnic forces.[19] The policing vacuum and Pentagon aversion to 'mission creep' also explained why indicted war criminals could move freely about *Republika Srpska* and the Croat-controlled areas of the Federation without concern for the 60,000 NATO troops – a condition of effective impunity that continued until the summer of 1997.[20] In effect, IFOR's commanders argued that to enforce the peace they needed to maintain the same position of 'impartiality' for which UNPROFOR commanders had been criticised during the war.[21]

This lacklustre enforcement of Dayton's provisions was greatly compounded by the fixation on a one-year 'exit strategy'. The time-limit was driven mainly by United States' political pressures, or to put it somewhat differently, by President Clinton's calculations of the limits of American public and congressional patience for the deployment. The problem was also aggravated by the Europeans' insistence that their troops would not stay in Bosnia one day longer than the Americans. The Clinton administration argued that setting a deadline of one year would in fact *help* the peace process by compelling the various protagonists, in effect, to take responsibility for their own future.[22] Subsequent experience showed this to be a serious miscalculation. The US focus on exit strategies significantly diminished the psychological climate of security that NATO troops could have provided from the very start. Nationalist leaderships were encouraged to wait out the international presence and prepare for partition or the resumption of war, while fear of resumed war encouraged voters to seek protection in their ethnic communities and leaderships. The most glaring case was *Republika Srpska*. Upon learning some two years later that the US troop deployment was to be extended indefinitely, Serb functionaries at every level became altogether more cooperative.[23]

Progress and stalemate

During these early years, the dramatic failure and collapse of Dayton Bosnia seemed as likely as anything else. That this worst case did not happen can be attributed to luck and learning. First, it is reasonable to speculate that the passage of two years permitted the most intense of the wartime animosities to subside. A marginally more acquiescent attitude on the part of the Bosnian Serb population coincided with greater determination by peace-implementing powers to enforce Dayton. Both the new Labour government under British Prime Minister Tony Blair and the Clinton administration showed a new willingness to take risks. Mid-level war-crimes suspects were captured and taken to The Hague. Radovan Karadzic had to flee his headquarters in Pale, which made it more difficult for him to run *Repubulika Srpska* as a private criminal fiefdom. NATO troops also seized Serb television transmitters (the day after *Republika Srpska* television broadcast film of SFOR soldiers spliced with newsreel footage of Nazi troops).

The United States continued to emphasise a balance-of-power approach based on building up its Muslim clients through the 'train-and-equip' programme. A peacetime equivalent of 'lift-and-strike', it provoked similar irritation among European allies who judged it, correctly, as driven by the American determination to leave Bosnia as soon as possible. However, once Washington decided to stay indefinitely, 'train and equip' did play a positive role: concentrating Serb minds on their real interest in avoiding another war. In early 1997, the Muslim leadership in Sarajevo was circulating a map showing what new territory they would demand to be part of a partitioned Bosnian state if Dayton – as seemed ever more likely – were to collapse.[24] With *Republika Srpska* receiving less than 2% of Bosnian reconstruction aid, 'hollowing out' demographically and facing freshly equipped Muslim forces, Bosnia's Serbs could reasonably conclude that they had an existential stake in the success of Dayton.

These were the circumstances in which Biljana Plavsic, Karadzic's former deputy turned figurehead president, decided to challenge his corrupt leadership and to lead *Republika Srpska* into a more cooperative relationship with Dayton's enforcers. Plavsic was a former biology professor and extreme Serb nationalist who would later find herself in custody at The Hague for her wartime activities.

But extreme or not, Plavsic was apparently a *genuine* nationalist – that is to say, a Serb patriot who started to reflect upon the sorry condition to which the Karadzic leadership had reduced her fellow Serbs. Plavsic moved herself and the *Republika Srpska* Assembly to Banja Luka, declaring it the capital and thereby challenging the Pale Serbs' grandiose pretensions to build a 'New Sarajevo'. She immediately received support and physical protection from NATO troops and the Office of the High Representative (OHR) – Bosnia's international administrator under Dayton. More successes, albeit modest ones, followed. The high-water mark of Bosnian Serb 'liberalisation' was the election in late 1997 of an anti-war liberal, Milorad Dodik, as Prime Minister of *Republika Srpska*. With only a thin majority in Bosnian Serb Assembly, Dodik depended on the votes of 16 Muslim deputies; their voting presence in the Assembly was itself a measure of progress.

The most remarkable success, arguably, was in an area long considered Dayton's greatest failure: refugee return. Through 1998, refugee returns to 'minority areas' – that is, areas dominated by a different ethnic group – were negligible, and the few returnees often faced organised local campaigns of violence. In 1999, however, a significant number of Muslims and Croats made their way back to the cleansed areas of *Republika Srpska*. Month-on-month comparisons showed that the rate of return had accelerated in early 2000.[25] These developments raised the possibility that sometime in the year 2003 it would be possible to declare that refugee return in Bosnia was substantially finished – that is to say, as complete as it would ever be. In Bosnia itself, as of summer 2000, there were 900,000 registered displaced persons. Various factors of over-counting suggest that the real figure maybe closer to 600,000. Historical experience suggests that one-third of these will return home, but in Bosnia it might be closer to a half, or 300,000 people. In any event, the refugee returns in Bosnia were already unprecedented compared to other post-war ethnic divides – such as in Cyprus. By 2002 there was, moreover, real freedom of movement and a notable absence of ethnic violence. Ethnic cleansing had not been reversed, but arguably its logic was eroding.

These surprising – but still modest – refugee returns suggested a modest way of measuring whether Dayton could be judged a 'success'. The best plausible scenario was neither formal partition nor a rapid restoration of the more attractive, multi-ethnic aspects of pre-war Bosnian society. It was, rather, a middle scenario in which three communities would coexist peacefully, in two separate entities but under a common – and commonly accepted – roof of a sovereign Bosnia and Herzegovina. In the medium term, the two entities would largely govern themselves. At the same time, the common institutions and overarching state sovereignty would provide shelter for those civic forces determined to resist fanatic nationalism. In the long run, with democratisation in Croatia and Serbia, an increasingly integrated Bosnian economy, a steadily improving functioning of both the Federation government and the common institutions of the Bosnian state, an open media and, above all, a gradual increase in refugee returns across ethnic lines, Bosnia's internal borders might gradually blur. Thus Dayton could be seen as a framework for eroding the tyranny of ethnicity over Bosnia's daily life.

As of late 2001, Bosnia had reached a stalemate that fell short even by this modest measure. The economy was criminalised, aid-dependent and stagnant. *Republika Srpska* had drifted back into the political sway of hard-line nationalists, notwithstanding the democratic changes in Serbia proper. Indeed, the election of a non-nationalist government in Croatia seems to have made hard-line Bosnian Croats even more intransigent: beleaguered by the cut-off of Zagreb's financial support, and threatened by a change in election rules designed to dilute the nationalists' voting bloc, they staged a mini-revolt, withdrawing from the common presidency and calling on Croatian members of the Federation Army to mutiny.

The implementing powers of Dayton had set up an odd kind of half-protectorate. International representatives had progressively assumed the formal authority, but not really the concrete powers, of colonial administrators. Presidents could be dismissed; unified vehicle licence plates and a new national flag could be imposed. But a police force trusted by all three communities could not easily be assembled, nor were the international powers able to fill the vacuum with their own police.

The goal of a viable, unified, self-governing state remained distant. This reality was underscored, rather than negated, by the election in 2000 of the first non-ethnically based coalition to assume leadership in both the Federation and national governments. The alliance found that it presided over only the shell of a state, with myriad boundaries and levels of authority, and with two formal (and three *de facto*) armies. It was a constitutional dysfunction that flowed from the genuinely difficult dilemma faced by the drafters of Dayton. They had granted the Muslims, Croats and Serbs effective blocking vetoes over issues of 'vital' interest to each of the three national groups. Aside from being demanded by the Serbs and Croats, this mechanism was arguably necessary to build confidence amid ethnic insecurity. Yet the consequence of such 'consociational' constitutions is almost invariably to freeze, rather than resolve conflicts.[26]

Six years after Dayton, the conflict was frozen still. Worse alternatives could be imagined, however. The operative question was not so much how soon could a viable Bosnian state be built, but rather, how long was NATO prepared to stay?

Chapter 3

Kosovo and the Struggle for Unity

NATO won its 78-day air war in June 1999 because it was able to convince one man that the alliance was united and serious about defeating him. Success came at a high cost, as emphasised by many critics of the war; and it came too late to forestall great tragedy, as emphasised by the many backers of the war who felt that a comparable use of force in 1992 could have averted much of the Yugoslav disaster.[1]

Slobodan Milosevic, the man who needed convincing, had been widely recognised at the outset of the decade as a central demagogue in the destruction of Yugoslavia. Yet he had reinvented himself, as an indispensable – if not much loved – Western partner: first, persuading the Bosnian Serb leadership to sign on to the Vance-Owen Peace Plan; then imposing a semi-serious blockade on them when they reneged; finally, and most importantly, representing Bosnian Serbs at Dayton and making critical concessions at key junctures in the negotiations. Western interlocutors were impressed, quite often in spite of themselves, by his formidable charm and beguiling pragmatism. He embodied a verity of Shakespeare ('That one may smile, and smile, and be a villain'), and constituted a case study of the role of individuals in history. The power of Milosevic's personality was another important factor confounding the quest for transatlantic unity.[2]

Paradoxically, however, by March 1999 it proved easier for the alliance as a whole to use sustained military force against the state and regime headed by Milosevic than against the more classical villains, Karadzic and Mladic. Moreover, NATO launched air strikes in opposition to much of world opinion, including that of Russia, China and India; without the legitimacy of a UN Security Council mandate; and in the face of Belgrade's recognised sovereignty over Kosovo.

What can explain NATO's unity around such a daunting intervention? The main answer is that the transatlantic allies had exhausted every plausible diplomatic means to contain a conflict whose expansion was rightly judged as intolerable to Europe's moral compact and internal order. It was also important that Milosevic himself was bereft, this time, of alibis. In contrast to the Bosnian war, there were in Kosovo no obfuscating layers of supposedly autonomous actors. His responsibility for the actions of police, army and interior-ministry forces (MUP) was direct and undeniable. His historical responsibility was also well understood. Kosovo, the geographical starting point of Yugoslavia's undoing, was the volatile fuel that Milosevic had ignited in order to ride the rocket of Serb nationalism.

In July 1990, after Belgrade abolished Kosovo's constitutional autonomy, Albanian provincial deputies declared the 'Republic of Kosovo' a sovereign entity within Yugoslavia; demonstrators took to the streets and miners went on strike. Belgrade reacted fiercely by imposing martial law with thousands of soldiers, reservists and special Interior Ministry forces. Arbitrary arrests, beatings and torture were common. Public institutions were Serbified; university professors, schoolteachers and hospital staff dismissed; newspapers and Albanian-language radio broadcasts shut down. At this point, Kosovo already might have suffered the same horrors as Bosnia. Instead of waging war, however, Albanians accepted the pacifist leadership of a literary critic turned politician, Ibrahim Rugova. Rugova directed a strategy of non-violent resistance to Serb control, together with the construction of a 'parallel state', financed by an Albanian diaspora in Western Europe and the United States, and grudgingly tolerated by Belgrade.

Given this restraint, when the Kosovars' non-violent strategy collapsed in the winter of 1998, it was not so difficult for the West to agree that Belgrade and especially Milosevic were to blame. To be sure, there was by this time an additional factor, the Kosovo Liberation Army (KLA), some elements of which were criminal in their organisation and terrorist in their strategy towards Serb civilians and Kosovar Albanian 'collaborators'. The KLA as a whole was in no mood to compromise. Therefore the Kosovo problem, inherently difficult to begin with, now was going to be nearly impossible to solve on the West's preferred terms, under which Kosovo would remain part of Yugoslavia. Having done so much to aggravate the problem, however, Milosevic had to show some evidence of trying to solve it, if he hoped to regain the indulgence of the West – or at least enough of the West to divide it again. Instead, what he offered throughout 1998 and into 1999 was a scorched-earth campaign directed mainly against Kosovar civilians.

Thus, the difficulties posed for NATO as it went to war for Kosovo were no longer so much of a *transatlantic* nature – that is to say, a clash of old- and new-world values, interests and strategic perspectives. Instead, NATO faced more universal dilemmas of intervention: of taking sides; of marrying force and diplomacy; of establishing legitimacy for the use of military force; and of waging war by consensus among diverse democracies. These dilemmas were difficult, with no good solutions. Yet hindsight confirms that, with a few important exceptions, NATO was able to pursue the least bad option.

Taking sides

One criticism of NATO's Kosovo intervention is that the alliance, under US leadership, allowed itself to be manipulated by the KLA into fighting a war of Kosovar secession. In taking sides militarily, the critique continues, NATO – especially the United States – inverted strategic logic. Against their own interests, the US and NATO promoted further ethnic fragmentation of rump Yugoslavia, and ruined relations with the major powers that really matter: Russia and China. In a trenchant version of this critique, Michael Mandelbaum labelled it the 'Albright legacy' to have focused 'the vast strength of American foreign policy on a tiny former Ottoman possession of no strategic importance or economic value, with which the United States had no ties of history, geography or sentiment'.[3] Fuelling such criticisms, on the American side, is fear that if Washington allows secessionist movements to manipulate the American debate through imagery and emotion, it will lose its strategic way in the world. There is no shortage of other secessionists hoping to draw the West into their fights.

It is true enough that NATO found itself using military force in the objective service of a cause that it opposed: Kosovo's *de facto* separation and, most likely, eventual independence from Serbia. Yet it is difficult to see how it could have avoided doing so. It certainly made an effort, until March 1999, to chart a middle course, condemning Belgrade's repression and suspension of autonomy but supporting Yugoslav sovereignty over the province. Early US policy toward Kosovo had been crafted to avoid inadvertently serving the Kosovar agenda. In December 1992, fearful that Bosnia-style carnage would have greater strategic implications if it spread to the south Balkans, the Bush administration delivered to Belgrade its so-called 'Christmas Warning'. It told Serbia that ethnic cleansing against Albanians would provoke a US military response, possibly against Serbia itself. However, the Americans also made clear to the Kosovo Albanians that they were on their own if *they* resorted to violence first.[4] For a long time, the careful calibration of this warning was never tested – largely because Rugova's entourage feared a blood–bath like Bosnia's; but also because they took this fine print in the Christmas Warning very seriously.[5] When the KLA started to gain the initiative, however, they were able to exploit the difficulties in this calibration. Would the US and its allies really excuse Serb atrocities, no matter how massive, if the Serbs were arguably responding to provocations, no matter how minor?

In any event, KLA provocations were not the main cause of the war. The West's central dilemma was, rather, how outside powers could insist on the integrity of Yugoslavia's borders when Belgrade was unwilling to create the conditions that would make them viable. This point requires some historical perspective. There is no denying that the historical element of Kosovar separatism posed its own problems, or that, before 1989, Serbs themselves had been subjected to a degree of persecution from the local Albanian majority that enjoyed significant autonomy under Tito's 1974 constitution.[6] Yet whatever else one wants to say about Titoist rule, it had made an effort to calm rather than inflame ethnic antagonisms. Milosevic, seeing that the exploitation of Serb grievances offered him a ladder to the political summit, climbed it. He took his cue from the taboo-breaking 1986 Memorandum of the Serbian Academy of Sciences and Arts, which had asserted that Kosovo Serbs have been victims of an Albanian 'genocide'. After Milosevic became head of Serbia's

League of Communists in 1986, he was able to place friends and allies into top jobs in the state press and broadcast media. A media that had once ranked among communist Europe's most open and professional became subverted into an instrument of hate propaganda targeted, in the first instance, against Kosovo's Albanians.[7] The emotive – and entirely fabricated – charge of widespread 'rape' was added to that of genocide.[8]

For their restraint through 1997, the Kosovars enjoyed consid– erable Western support. In retrospect, however, it is hard to avoid the conclusion that both the Rugova strategy, combining pacifist tactics and maximalist demands, and the Western posture of supporting Rugova but not his aspirations, were untenable. Time was not on the side of a peaceful solution. The settlement ending the Bosnian war had a powerful and overwhelmingly negative knock- on effect in Kosovo. Even before the Dayton agreement, pressures were building for a more confrontational strategy. Dayton intensified these pressures for two reasons: because it showed that Bosnian Serb violence, compared to Kosovar Albanian non-violence, brought results (an internationally recognised *Republika Srpska*); and because it suggested the regional road to partition, with separatist ethnic communities moving toward union with their 'mother' countries across the border. A core of dissidents from the League of Democratic Kosova (or LDK, Rugova's party) line started to argue publicly that Rugova's strategy had failed and that it was time to organise mass demonstrations and a more aggressive campaign of civil disobedience.[9] The KLA – an organisation whose very existence was being disputed as late as fall 1997 – took up armed resistance, staging sporadic attacks against Serb police and civilians, and against Albanian 'collaborators'. It started raising recruits and money – at the expense of the LDK – in Germany, Switzerland and the United States. Neighbouring Albania's spring 1997 descent into anarchy helped immeasurably, as much of the vast arsenal of light weapons 'liberated' in that meltdown made its way to Kosovo.

Serbs themselves were the authors of the event that turned an armed-resistance movement into a province-wide insurrection. In early March 1998, Serb special police launched an attack against the family compound of Adem Jashari, a KLA-allied brigand, in the village of Drenica. At least 80 Albanians died, including dozens of women and children. Outraged villagers across Kosovo took up arms, seizing villages and taking control of strategic highways as startled Serb forces fell back in disarray. With little overall command and, therefore, no strategic plan for actually holding on to the positions they had taken, the Kosovars were vulnerable to a Serb counter-attack with heavy weapons. Once organised, the counter-offensive sent the KLA reeling. Serb security forces employed a strategy that was brutal but effective: shell, burn and depopulate villages, depriving the guerrillas not only of cover but of fighters too, as men from the razed villages made it their first priority to care for their displaced families.[10]

At this point, in the summer of 1998, there was already a strong case for Western military intervention. Serb 'scorched-earth' tactics were not only morally obnoxious but were also driving tens of thousands of refugees into neighbouring Albania and Macedonia, with destabilising consequences for both countries. Moreover, the fundamental Western interest was to demonstrate effective support for the more moderate Kosovar leadership, and thus keep alive the possibility of a compromise settlement short of independence. And there were still some prominent Kosovars willing to discuss, for example, a solution under which Kosovo would have become one of three republics in a reorganised rump Yugoslavia. However, such options were disappearing – the inevitable consequence of the deteriorating situation on the ground. By the standards of the West's Bosnia experience, NATO resorted quickly – within four months of the Drenica massacre – to issuing threats of military intervention. However, NATO leaders now found themselves hemmed in by the unwelcome consequences of practically any policy course they might take. Leaning on Rugova to moderate his demands, or to meet with Milosevic, only discredited him while boosting the KLA's prestige.[11] Allowing the KLA to be brought down a notch through military defeat – as happened during the summer of 1998 – proved a moral disaster as hundreds of thousands were driven and burned out of their homes. Making good on the threat of air strikes would have given cover to the KLA to continue a war of secession that NATO opposed.

After Bosnia, this was becoming a familiar problem: the immense difficulty of intervening to end a war without taking sides. There was no good way around this dilemma. But standing passively in the face of Belgrade's scorched-earth campaign finally proved untenable. By October 1998, the fighting had created more than 200,000 refugees within Kosovo: tens of thousands without shelter as winter approached, and many more in damaged houses that would not see them through. The province was strewn with the carcasses of livestock deliberately killed by Serb forces, for no apparent reason other than making it more difficult for Kosovo Albanians to feed themselves.[12] The approaching Balkan winter portended a humanitarian catastrophe. The crisis finally galvanised a NATO consensus for air strikes against Yugoslavia in October 1998. The 16 NATO members approved an 'activation order' – giving SACEUR General Wesley Clark the authority to launch strikes without further formal approval – despite continued Russian opposition on the Security Council, widespread wariness of the precedent involved in challenging Belgrade's recognised sovereignty and great uncertainty about the connection between military targets and political consequences.

Force and diplomacy

Bombing was averted by Milosevic's eleventh-hour climb-down, but the air campaign that began five months later had been set in motion, in effect, by that October activation order. This sequence has led to another accusation about NATO's intervention: that it was somehow engineered by officials in Washington, who never believed in a peaceful settlement and who used the intervening five months to orchestrate a set of bogus negotiations, featuring an ultimatum so grievously offensive to the Serbs' national dignity and sovereignty that they had no choice but to refuse.

This accusation is false. Paris and London were as determined to stop Serb atrocities as was Washington; it is not, in any event, consistent with the French understanding of alliance obligations to allow oneself to be railroaded into an American-led war. What ensued was hardly the first campaign of ethnic cleansing that Milosevic had presided over, and that ethnic cleansing, whatever its antecedents, says something about whether Belgrade was negotiating in good faith. A more serious question is whether the Western allies, having learned the lessons of Bosnia, employed the threat of force effectively in the service of diplomacy. Here the best answer available is that they employed the threat prudently. The diplomacy failed, and war was the result, so in literal terms one must conclude that diplomacy and the threat of force were not wedded effectively. The main problem was not over-eagerness, however, but a reluctance to use force that was too obvious to both Serbs and Albanians.

The consequences of this reluctance could be seen in the October agreement that Richard Holbrooke negotiated with Milosevic. Belgrade promised to withdraw substantial numbers of security forces, to allow the deployment of 2,000 unarmed OSCE 'verifiers' to monitor a cease-fire and to negotiate the details of a restored autonomy for the province. The agreement had two main virtues. First, it addressed the most acute emergency – bringing refugees down from the hills to be fed and kept warm. Second, in making the agreement and accepting the dispatch of 2,000 monitors, Milosevic made a critical concession: in effect, the territory of Kosovo was 'internationalised' – a status that the Rugova had been seeking for years. While there were worries that the 'verifiers' would become hostages – useful for Belgrade in deterring the next NATO threat – they in fact made the West hostage to resolving the conflict, one way or another.

Clearly Milosevic would not have agreed to as much if not for the NATO threat of military action. Still, the pact was a rickety affair. Missing was any provision for an outside security force, such as in Bosnia, that both sides would respect and perhaps even trust. But NATO was not ready to bomb for such a force, and Holbrooke could not convincingly demand it – especially given resistance in the Pentagon and Republican-controlled Congress to deploying American peacekeepers in Kosovo. The result was a pre-programmed disaster: Serbs were allowed to maintain roughly 10,000 police and 11,000 army troops in Kosovo; while the KLA, in practice, was able to reoccupy positions from which it had just been driven and prepare for resumption of war in the spring. Amid mutual provocations, the Serb security forces' massacre of 40 Albanians – including fleeing women and children – outside the village of Racak brought matters to a head.

In response to Racak, the Contact Group intensified its diplomacy. Serbs and Albanians were summoned to talks at a French castle near Rambouillet. To persuade the Serbs to come, NATO issued a second ultimatum to Belgrade, problematic for those who recalled that an integral part of the Serb national myth has involved standing up to ultimatums from Vienna in 1914, Nazi Germany in 1941 and Stalin in 1948.[13] But NATO had no real choice: a prime purpose of its diplomacy was to convince the Kosovar Albanians that, if they returned to peaceful methods which had, up to then, proved unavailing, the West could deliver them self-government. This purpose required also dealing with the KLA, whom some American and European officials had labelled 'terrorists'. And reconciling the various Albanian factions to one another was a difficult task. Not only did the KLA reject Rugova's strategy, but among guerrilla commanders there was a deep-seated antipathy to his entire entourage – many of them Tito-era provincial officials who had been responsible for jailing Albanian nationalists in the 1970s and 1980s. Moreover, the KLA itself was divided and almost structureless: a group of independent commanders struggling to stay out in front of what constituted, at times, a spontaneous insurrection. Thus, it was a major accomplishment that, in the week before Rambouillet, the Kosovars were able, with the help of US Ambassador to Macedonia Christopher Hill, to constitute a broad delegation, including KLA political chief, Hashim Thaci.

The draft settlement presented to the Serbs at Rambouillet had evolved in a direction broadly favourable to the Albanians.[14] It reflected the reality that the Kosovars could not be persuaded to accept a status of autonomy that left them administratively subordinate to Serbia. It returned the basic powers that Kosovo had enjoyed under the 1974 constitution, and left no obligatory links to Serbia. There did remain some links to the Yugoslav federation, but in effect, the Rambouillet draft settlement constituted the clear beginning of a 'disassociation' from the Yugoslav framework.[15] On the question of final status, the plan promised a 'mechanism' that would take into account the 'will of the people' after three years.[16] A separate letter from Madeleine Albright to Thaci indicated that the 'mechanism' would include a referendum.

Though a very good deal for the Kosovar Albanians, Rambouillet was also the best deal that the Serbs themselves could have hoped to achieve. It included several levels of 'positive discrimination' in favour of the Serb minority, including a disproportionate representation in the Kosovo parliament, and a clause – familiar in earlier Yugoslav constitutions – that no law touching on Serb 'vital interests' could be automatically passed against the opposition of a majority of Serb deputies.[17] Serbs did not get the second parliamentary chamber that they sought, but they did win the concession that legal disputes between Serbs could be tried by courts in Serbia. Most importantly, it contained a commitment by the KLA to end their rebellion and disarm, and to give up claims to immediate independence.

The real stumbling block was Belgrade's refusal to accept the presence of a NATO military force to guarantee the constitutional and political arrangements. Neither the Albanians nor the West could agree to anything less. The Albanians, who had long sought this kind of 'militarised protectorate', were hardly ready to trust Serb security forces after their conduct of the preceding 13 months. And the West could see now that any settlement without a credible outside security force would be just a warmed-over version of the October agreement, sure to suffer the same fate. This Western realisation had been accompanied by a greater sense of transatlantic realism about what was required, with the British and French taking the lead in planning a Kosovo peace implementation force under French command, and the Clinton administration conceding that US troops would have to take part.

In a sense then, NATO's Kosovo war resulted from Belgrade's defiance of a third ultimatum: accept a NATO force that would attenuate (to say the least) Yugoslavia's effective sovereignty; or be bombed. After the first round of talks were suspended on 23 February, the Albanian delegates committed themselves in principle to the document, but said that they needed to consult their various constituencies in Kosovo before signing. It was certainly their understanding that if they signed by 15 March, the peace plan became non-negotiable.[18] The infamous military appendix to Rambouillet contained provisions that were undoubtedly obnoxious to Serb national feeling – such as NATO over-flights of Serbia proper, and even the free use of Serb military facilities.[19] And it is true enough that the United States, at least, was going to be unyielding about the fundamentals of a robust NATO presence in Kosovo and a complete Serb withdrawal from the territory.

It is true also that certain US officials, in particular, expected the negotiations to fail. Nevertheless, the accusation that the United States was hell-bent on war is a cartoon version of events. It was Milosevic who refused to discuss the military annex, using the legal technicality that it was not a 'Contact Group' document. 'To be sure, we weren't in a negotiating mood [either]', recalled Hill, the US negotiator.

> But if he had come back to us and said, 'I accept the force, but…', we would have listened to the 'but'. He could have put us in a difficult position by saying, 'I accept the force, but no president of Kosovo, and no different legal system'. Or if he said, 'I accept the force, but demand full sanctions relief'. Or, 'let me into PfP'. What were we going to do – bomb him because he wants into PfP? We couldn't have bombed him if he had done any of these things. But he just didn't want the force … If Milosevic had agreed to engage on the annex, some of the language would have been negotiable. The fact is, he refused to engage in discussing a single word … For three weeks after Rambouillet, instead of preparing his people to accept peace, [Milosevic] prepared for war.[20]

The problem of legitimacy

The most potent criticisms of NATO's Kosovo intervention are that the war was illegal under international law; a violation of Belgrade's recognised sovereignty over Kosovo; damaging to a UN-regulated system for authorising the use of force; and thereby dangerously unsettling to international relations in general. This 'legitimacy' argument does not rest on denying the fact of Serb brutality toward Kosovar civilians; indeed, the heart of the argument is that some evils must be accepted for the sake of a broader order.

There is abundant evidence that the argument was grounded, for the most part, in genuine alarm on the part of governments that US-led 'vigilantism' threatens global stability and their own legitimate interests. India's protests were perhaps mostly rhetorical and laden with residual anti-Americanism, but Delhi does have reason to worry, in Kashmir and elsewhere, about the principle of outside intervention on behalf of aggrieved populations.[21] China had more direct reason to fear the possible precedent for US intervention on behalf of the Chinese 'province' of Taiwan (and this before the fiasco of NATO's mistaken bombing of Beijing's embassy in Belgrade, with loss of three Chinese lives).

The most serious concern was Russia's. On the substance of the Kosovo dispute, Russian diplomacy through summer 1998 had been in line with that of other members of the Contact Group, contradicting much casual commentary about a significant Russian attachment to a Slav-Orthodox axis. When it came to air strikes, however, Moscow seemed truly alarmed at the prospect of NATO military action beyond its members' borders. For NATO to act without a Security Council mandate implied a devaluation of one of Moscow's last remaining Great Power platforms. And after Moscow had grudgingly accepted NATO enlargement to Central Europe, the Kosovo air campaign could only reinforce Russian awareness of how constricted its strategic space had become. As one Moscow analyst put it: 'All we know is that in a period of one month, NATO took in three new members, finished its New Strategic Concept, and went to war against Yugoslavia'.[22] A member of the Russian State Duma asked, 'Who can guarantee that, if not Russia, then somebody else close to Russia will not be punished in the same way?'.[23]

Russians were sensitive to parallels between the Serbs whom Yugoslavia's break-up stranded outside their national state and the 25 million Russians left 'homeless' by the demise of the Soviet Union. They worried about Islamist fanaticism, while the prospect of Kosovo's independence brought to mind Russia's own federal fragility. The KLA reminded many Russians of Chechen 'brigands'. A Russian analyst described the sum of all these fears:

> *Few people in Russia believe that NATO undertook its military action in response to a humanitarian catastrophe. On the contrary, the widespread view is that NATO instigated instability by supporting the Kosovo Liberation Army and other extremist forces as a pretext to further split up Yugoslavia – the only country in the region not aspiring to join the alliance – and to increase its military presence in the Balkans.*[24]

That such views are well detached from reality does not make them disingenuous. Nor does Russia's uneven adherence to UN and OSCE standards (Russian conduct in Chechnya being just one example) diminish the likelihood that Moscow sees itself, in a weakened and beleaguered state, as having a substantial stake in international legal norms governing the use of force. Those who criticise NATO's Kosovo intervention on legal grounds worry that the long-term consequences will include undermining this Russian stake.

This Russian reaction heightened the anxieties among various NATO members about the legitimacy of their action. The consensus for air strikes, in March 1999 as well as for the earlier Activation Order of October 1998, did not diminish the reality of fundamental allied disagreements about acting without a UN mandate. The American view, shared to a lesser extent by the British, was that legitimacy should not be confused with the formal mandate of a UN Security Council that is too divided, and in other ways unqualified, to judge that legitimacy. Rather, protecting Albanian civilians from Serb brutalities was inherently legitimate, grounded in moral principle and a revived tradition of humanitarian law.[25] The French government took the view that while a UN mandate for military intervention should be required in principle, the humanitarian emergency justified violating that rule in practice. Germany and Italy, 'civilian' powers with deep cultural and constitutional inhibitions about using force anyway, were the most troubled by the precedent being set.

But the general sense was that the outrages of Bosnia could not be tolerated again in the European space. And Belgrade, of course, made it easy for NATO to agree on and justify its intervention. The vast ethnic cleansing of Kosovo was organised and systematic; it repeated the pattern of killings and expulsions that marked the onset of Serb attacks in both Croatia and Bosnia – down to the dispatching of paramilitary thugs such as Zeljko Raznatovic's 'Arkan' ('Tigers') to sow terror among Albanian civilians. Within days, hundreds of thousands of deportees had been deposited at the Albanian and Macedonian borders; within weeks it was nearly a million. There is, in fact, an international obligation to take action against genocide, and genocide was a word that US and UK officials applied, consciously and deliberately, early in the war.[26] That the level of killings arguably did not turn out to justify the label is not the only consideration (an early Hague tribunal estimate was 11,334).[27] By the first week of April 1999, it certainly looked like it could be genocide; it was being conducted by a regime that had been involved in a programme of near genocide in Croatia and Bosnia, and waiting until genocide was a proven, accomplished fact would mean, of course, failing to prevent it. And whatever the real proportions of murdered, terrorised and expelled, the act of driving out an entire ethnic population makes one thing very clear: in Milosevic's Kosovo there was no place for Albanians. If the inter–national community was not willing to accept that proposition, then it had to embrace its opposite: Belgrade through its actions had forfeited its sovereignty over the province.

To be sure, NATO went to war for a mixture of reasons. Hill, the US envoy, has argued:

> *We did not go to war over Rambouillet. We went to war because [Milosevic] started ethnic cleansing. He sent in 40,000 troops to intimidate the Albanians and to intimidate us.*[28]

This statement is reasonable but somewhat problematic. Its larger truth is that the NATO consensus to bomb had been forged by a Serb scorched-earth campaign that started in early 1998, and was resuming in the week before 24 March 1999. Its problem is that NATO had committed itself to launch air strikes if Milosevic did not accept something very close to the Rambouillet agreement. The KLA had agreed to end its insurrection on the basis of this promise. Making good on this moral commitment was perhaps the last chance to reconcile the Albanians to a Western-backed solution. This was a strong reason, but it somewhat undercuts the idea that NATO responded only to massive ethnic cleansing.

It also may be true that the bombing caused Belgrade to accelerate its campaign, hoping to depopulate Kosovo of its Albanian majority before being forced to settle. Proponents of military inter–vention are at a disadvantage if they want to suggest that war will have a positive effect on political dynamics in the short term. War, as Adam Roberts has observed, means moral chaos, almost by definition:

> *All major cases of genocide and ethnic cleansing in the twentieth century have occurred during or immediately after major wars: the chaos and hatred unleashed in war, and the secrecy that wartime conditions engender, can provide the necessary conditions for mass cruelty.*[29]

In strict terms, Belgrade's earlier Kosovo campaign of summer 1998 was not 'ethnic cleansing' – that is, not an attempt to redraw the ethnic map by killing and expelling one population to replace it with another. Yet, it is now clear that this was Belgrade's version of 'restrained' action. From early June 1998, NATO governments had put Milosevic on notice that they were preparing to intervene if Serb conduct crossed an (unspecified) threshold. Serb forces seemed to take care to stay just under what was calculated to be the level of brutality that NATO could swallow. Hence a paradox: NATO threats had prevented ethnic cleansing. At some point, NATO had to make good on the threat, or the threat became useless. Making good, however, removed the restraint, and therefore might be considered the proximate trigger of mass cleansing. At this point, NATO had no choice but to defeat the agents of that campaign.

War by committee

NATO was not prepared to fight a war. Its members had achieved a consensus for something else: to threaten air strikes and, if necessary, to carry out the threat. There was some hope that Milosevic would relent, once convinced by several days of bombing that the alliance was serious.

Much criticism of the air campaign has focussed on this 'coercive' rather than effectively military function. The initial bombing campaign, while hardly 'pinprick', was limited to military targets in Kosovo and the Yugoslav-wide air-defence system. It was hampered by bad weather, a problem magnified by a scrupulous determination to avoid civilian casualties, and by the countervailing concern to avoid NATO casualties, which meant flying bombing missions at heights greater than 4,500 metres. It was hampered psychologically by statements from allied leaders – most importantly President Clinton – that a NATO ground campaign was not contemplated.

Gradually, as Belgrade showed no signs of relenting, the air campaign was ratcheted up to near 'strategic' levels, targeting such civilian–military 'dual-use' infrastructure as the Serb power grid. Key allied capitals also started to signal that, if all else failed, a ground campaign might have to be launched after all. Yet it is easy to see that this graduated escalation – both of the bombing and the rhetoric – invited the Milosevic regime to calculate that it might ride out the air campaign until NATO's consensus, presumed to be wobbly, fell apart. Based on the Serbs' previous experience in Bosnia, it was not implausible to imagine that NATO would settle for something less than its maximum demands. Meanwhile, Milosevic appears to have gambled that he could present the West with the *fait accompli* of a least a million fewer Albanians in Kosovo.

With ethnic cleansing on this vast scale, Belgrade achieved a strategic coup. For days and weeks, NATO leaders appeared shell-shocked. British officials admitted that a moral 'failure of imagination' had left them unprepared for a Serb strategy that seemed, in retrospect, all too predictable. NATO had no military options for directly countering the atrocities and deportations, and its limited forces in Albania and Macedonia (deployed in preparation for an eventual peace-keeping force) struggled to help relief agencies cope with the human misery. Beyond the misery, there was an immediate threat – as Belgrade no doubt intended – to regional stability. The 'demographic bomb' of 241,000 Albanian refugees added tensions to the unsteady ethnic relations in Macedonia, where state collapse looked like a real prospect. Montenegro, Serbia's increasingly independent sister republic with a history of good Slav–Albanian relations, also found the influx of 63,000 Albanian refugees to be politically unsettling. Throughout most of the air campaign, Belgrade had every reason to be encouraged that the alliance would checkmate itself. NATO strategy was set by consensus among 19 members, many of which were, in turn, trying to hold together internal consensus among their own divided governments and societies. Overall, the bombing campaign was phenomenally accurate, but each inevitable mishap, resulting in gruesome killings of civilians, strained the consensus.

All of this seemed the perfect recipe for strategic incoherence. NATO waged its war from 4,500 metres, hoping to pulverise the Serbian military and infrastructure until the Serbs gave up. That there was no historical precedent for victory on this basis could not trump the reality that NATO's democracies – most importantly the United States – had no stomach for the ground war that *could* ensure victory. (The single exception, Britain, was also the only major NATO power not stymied in its conduct of the war by a divided or coalition government.) Belgrade, meanwhile, continued to wage its own war on the ground against Kosovar civilians. The connection between NATO's war and Belgrade's war looked tenuous.

In retrospect, however, it is clear that NATO's problems were second-order liabilities, compared to the real disunity of purpose that the alliance had experienced for more than three years in Bosnia. Precisely *because* of the previous Bosnia experience, there was strong support for the Kosovo intervention in the United States, France and especially Britain. Weaker links were Germany, Italy and, above all, Greece. Yet, considered in historical context, Germany was in fact remarkably supportive of the war; its pilots were flying combat missions over Kosovo just a few years after a wrenching constitutional debate about whether Germans should ever again fight for anything but territorial defence. Foreign Minister Joschka Fischer, leader of the mainly pacifist Greens, was an eloquent exponent of the argument that it would constitute a perverse historical alibi to invoke Nazi crimes as a reason not to protect Albanians from similar crimes. And the SPD Chancellor, Gerhard Schröder, warned his newly installed centre-left government that the commitment to NATO remained central to Germany's *raison d'etat*. Italy too had to perform a delicate balance – its coalition government of ex-communists and former Christian Democrats depended for its majority on unreformed Communists who opposed the war. But governments come and go frequently in Rome, and Italy's allies could reasonably expect that this one would let itself fall before withdrawing its support. Even Greece's government, facing a furiously pro-Serb electorate, seemed more daunted by the prospect that, if Athens were to fall from alliance grace, the Aegean would become a lonely place to face Turkey's military might.

The alliance was thus stronger than it looked. Moreover, Belgrade's great strategic surprise was also its greatest miscalculation. Precisely the scale of the ethnic cleansing made it impossible for the alliance to disunite on the fundamental objective of reversing it. The mass deportation of Albanians played the same role in galvanising Western unity over Kosovo as the Srebrenica massacre had performed in Bosnia. As with Srebrenica, the Serb leadership in Belgrade suffered its own failure of imagination in not comprehending the threshold it had crossed for the West.

Much of the subsequent debate about the effectiveness of air power over Yugoslavia, while no doubt important to the planning of future campaigns, is beside the point when it comes to explaining how this one ended. NATO did not defeat Serb forces on the ground: it was a largely intact Yugoslav Army that withdrew between 9 and 20 June.[30] In the two years that followed, no new evidence added significantly to what can be adduced about why Milosevic capitulated. Four factors seem most plausible.

Firstly, the indictment of Milosevic and other top military and political leaders by the Hague war-crimes tribunal probably made it more difficult for NATO to compromise, and helped convince Milosevic that he could not negotiate a settlement ambiguous enough to capture some of his own aims. Secondly, Russia decided, for a variety of reasons, that it had little to gain and much to lose from continuing to support Belgrade in its defiance. German diplomacy played a critical role in nudging Moscow toward this decision by backing a G-8 set of principles slightly different in nuance, but essentially the same in substance as NATO's own demands. Thirdly, the decision to the target critical 'dual-use' (that is, civilian as well as military) infrastructure, most importantly the Yugoslav power grid, finally brought the war home to the average Serb. Finally, perhaps most important were signals from the United States that it would mount a ground invasion after all if it proved necessary – and it was starting to look unavoidable. These signals had the important subsidiary effect of reinforcing Moscow's interest in seeing the war end quickly.[31] The war ended in the way allied governments had expected it to end, with Milosevic realising that the alliance was serious about defeating him.

NATO transformed?

NATO prevailed, but its victory was traumatic: a 'near-death experience' that allies on both sides of the Atlantic seemed determined to avoid repeating. For the United States, the Kosovo war underscored the unwelcome political constraints that coalition warfare can impose on military operations. While target selection was almost exclusively American (and indeed, some operations went outside NATO channels altogether), target *approval* was a multilateral process involving 15 members. The process was tedious and contentious. US military commanders – notably General Michael Short who, as commander of Allied Air Forces Southern Europe, had direct operational control of air operations – were impatient from the outset with the limited effectiveness of strikes at Serb forces in Kosovo. Unable to force Belgrade's early capitulation, the US wanted to vastly expand the target list and to combine tactical with 'strategic' attacks against bridges, refining capacity, television and communications centres, and power stations throughout Yugoslavia. The Americans were frustrated, in part, because their initial list contained only a few days' worth of targets anyway, but mainly by strong European, especially French, reluctance to escalate.[32]

The Americans had a point, insofar as the entire campaign was an act of strategic coercion which perhaps required a massive psychological shock to Serbian society. But if the reluctance to escalate arguably prolonged the war, it is just as likely that France's selective veto of targets saved NATO's effort from moral embarrass-ment and even, perhaps, political collapse. Consider two targets: a television station that was bombed and a bridge that was spared. The American determination to destroy the central Yugoslav transmission studio, unquestionably a source of odious propaganda, was resisted by Paris on the grounds that it was a civilian facility. When the US finally got its way, the bombing of the studio killed 16 civilians (whom the Milosevic regime probably sacrificed intentionally).[33] Since Yugoslav television was back on the air within three hours, it is unclear what NATO accomplished except to aid the very propaganda that it was trying to fight. France persisted in vetoing a strike on the Belgrade bridge that was the site of nightly celebrations by revellers wearing 'target' tee-shirts. After the war, General Short publicly castigated Paris for this, calling it a mistake to allow the Serbs to treat the war, in effect, as a party.[34] Yet, moral and legal considerations aside, the political consequences of killing those civilian revellers intentionally could have been devastating to NATO's unity. The larger point is that this was a political war, using political as well as military means. The war entailed testing the limits of the laws of armed conflict: for in the attempt to coerce an entire society, the rigorous distinction between legitimate military and illegitimate non-military targets became blurred to a worrying degree.[35] Yet the intervention could not have been sustained if political limits (including limits on civilian or dual-use targets) had been ignored. The North Atlantic Council's micro-management of targeting, however unwelcome to the Pentagon, helped ensure that those limits were carefully considered.

For European allies, on the other hand, the Kosovo war was an unwelcome reminder of their utter dependence on US military assets and leadership. Thus, both the war and the diplomatic brink–

manship leading up to it inspired a remarkable consensus – with Britain for first time out in front – on the need for a new degree of defence autonomy built around the EU. But the Kosovo campaign, which was overwhelmingly American in terms of military assets employed, also underscored how very far the Europeans had to go if they wanted to develop any significant measure of defence autonomy.

The Kosovo experience also inspired some new mythology. Some European critics, noting the extreme US reluctance to plan for a ground invasion, argued that the Americans had, in effect, forced upon the Europeans a strategy that was ineffective and even cowardly: bombing from 4,500 metres. This is less than half true. Only the UK was clearly ready to deploy ground forces, and there was even some merit to the White House argument that early talk of a ground invasion could have driven at least Germany and Italy out of the coalition. But it is true that London's frustration with American reluctance to plan publicly for a ground invasion added plausibility to the argument that Europeans could not afford to remain constrained by the US assessment of its own interests. This frustration had started to build up well before NATO went to war. In effect, the question of a humanitarian intervention in Europe had to wait on the outcome of a political and interagency debate in Washington. The Pentagon was generally opposed to threatening (much less carrying out) an intervention; the State Department argued in favour; the White House stood in between; the whole debate was affected by the bitterness of congressional–executive relations during the impeachment drive against the president.[36] There is no reason to believe that an EU coalition – even if it had the military means – could have intervened earlier and more effectively: its method of decision-making and unity of purpose is even more fractious than that of the US, which is a single country after all. But the EU's interests are more directly involved.

The EU's December 1999 'headline goal' – a commitment to be 'able, by 2003, to deploy within 60 days and sustain for at least one year military forces of up to 50,000–60,000 persons' – grew directly out of the Europeans' manifest incapacity to wield adequate military forces on their own in Kosovo. Europe's leaders seemed determined not to find themselves in a position of such dependency again. Parliaments, however, did not stampede to boost defence budgets. If the measure of capabilities implied by the headline goal was being able to wage the equivalent of a Kosovo war on their own, then it seemed that the EU states were unlikely to meet their self-imposed deadline.[37]

Still, the terrorist attacks of September 2001, and the consequent war in Afghanistan, made the matter all the more urgent by underscoring once again a practical transatlantic division of responsibilities. The US military, with Kosovo on its mind, did not want another NATO-run campaign: this would have been illogical anyway, given that it was not a 'political' war requiring political legitimisation, but rather a war of self-defence against a clear enemy. The irony was considerable, given the efforts that the United States had put into promoting a counter-terrorist agenda in the various iterations in the 1990s of NATO's 'Strategic Concept'. NATO was to invoke Article 5 for the first time in its history in response to a terrorist event several thousand kilometres distant from Europe. Yet the net effect of a real war against terrorism, when it came, was to reinforce NATO's main role as a strictly 'European' security organisation.[38] It also reinforced the reality that NATO's European members could not always count on the United States (with more pressing engagements elsewhere) being ready or able to provide that security.

So while early success in meeting the headline goals looked improbable, long-term failure remained unpalatable. Given the Europeans' success in meeting the primary goals they have set themselves in 50 years of integration, failure in the defence field should not be assumed.

Chapter 4

The Western Alliance and its Balkan Protectorates

The immediate consequences of NATO's Kosovo victory were mixed. In Kosovo itself, there was a period of near anarchy. Withdrawal of Serb security forces was followed by Albanian revenge killings and the wholesale flight of Kosovo Serbs. KLA commanders started seizing power at the local level; moderate Albanian leaders had their own lives threatened.

Regionally, however, the post-war dynamics were more encouraging. Croatian elections that followed President Franjo Tudjman's death in 1999 turned his authoritarian, corrupt and fiercely nationalistic party, the Croatian Democratic Union, or HDZ, out of office. Most dramatically, in the fall of 2000, Milosevic was toppled in presidential elections; within a year he was delivered to The Hague war-crimes tribunal to face charges that included crimes against humanity and genocide. Political change in Serbia had not been a direct goal of the intervention, but arguably it was one result. It did not drive the Serbs to greater extremes of anti-Western nationalism: in the year after the Kosovo war, a majority had apparently come to recognise Milosevic, not NATO, as the prime author of their misfortunes.[1] Montenegro had already separated itself, *de facto*, from Belgrade's rule, drawing as far as it could under an ambiguous NATO security umbrella. Liberalisations in Croatia, Serbia and Montenegro were linked to a fairly consistent Western policy of denying the legitimacy and benefits of integration with the West for those countries that disregarded the sovereignty of Bosnia and political freedoms within their own borders. It had to be judged a success of Western policies that these three former Yugoslav republics, when confronted with this choice, chose the long (and uncertain) path to European integration.

A balance sheet also requires a realistic assessment of what might have happened in the absence of intervention. Most likely, there would have been repeated re-negotiations of the Holbrooke–Milosevic agreement, each version being violated as the last had been. There almost certainly would have been continued fighting between Serb forces and the KLA, with Serb forces at levels well above agreed ceilings. Belgrade would have continued, probably for years, a war directed mainly against Kosovar civilians: partly because it did not know any other way to fight; and partly because, as has now been demonstrated, there was a readiness and a plan to depopulate Kosovo of most or all of its Albanians. The effects on NATO unity and regional stability would have been disastrous, with hundreds of thousands of refugees driven into neighbouring countries, having little prospect of a return home, polarising Macedonian ethnic relations and creating a *de facto* KLA mini-state in northern Albania and perhaps western Macedonia. Thus, the first justification for NATO's bombing campaign is not that it toppled Milosevic or resolved the underlying conflict, but that it staved off greater disaster.

Inevitably, however, the interventions in Bosnia as well as Kosovo will be judged on how the alliance manages the two *de facto* protectorates that resulted. And the subsequent, more limited diplomatic engagement and military deployments in Macedonia provide a further test. While some problems are simply beyond the West's control, the alliance demonstrated in Kosovo and Macedonia that it could avoid the corrosive disunity that proved so confounding during the Bosnian war. Possible future threats to that unity fall into three categories: continuing conflicts; post-war administrations; and long-term strategies.

Continuing conflicts

Milosevic obviously will be survived by some of the ethnic tensions that he aggravated, particularly in the south Balkans between Albanians and Slavs. As the alliance grapples with the issues at the heart of these tensions – including Kosovo's final status and the implications for Macedonia – there are bound to be transatlantic differences of emphasis if not of principle.

The KLA

From the first days of the Kosovo war, as the enormity of ethnic cleansing became apparent, Albanian retaliation against innocent Serbs was easy enough to predict.[2] The viciousness of the payback was nonetheless shocking. In the first weeks after the Serb capitulation, the tide of revenge went more or less unchecked in a security vacuum that NATO military forces were unable to fill. UN police were too late, too few and inadequately trained. The ensuing lawlessness was a general condition, in large measure apolitical, victimising Albanians as well as Serbs. There is no doubt, however, that Serbs (and other non-Albanian minorities) were special targets.

This grim situation was not yet a matter of serious policy disagreement. But there was a degree of transatlantic tension stemming from the suspicions of many Europeans that the United States had invited inevitable 'blowback' from the KLA, which it embraced before and during the bombing. It is true that the United States led efforts to create a common Albanian negotiating front which – as American officials saw it – had to include the KLA. These efforts intensified at Rambouillet, where US State Department spokesman James Rubin struck up a personal rapport with Thaci, the KLA political chief.[3] This relationship laid the basis for Secretary of State Madeleine Albright's direct assurances to Thaci that if he signed Rambouillet, the agreement's three-year 'review' mechanism would include a referendum on Kosovo's final status. During the war, the KLA provided NATO with intelligence about Serb forces through Albanian government intermediaries.[4] At the war's end, NATO gave direct air support to Albanian guerrillas struggling to hold on to Mount Pastrik on a vital KLA supply route near the Albanian border.

The KLA was the only force to face Serbs soldiers on the ground, and afterwards its leaders clearly expected their reward in the form of substantial political influence, if not control, over an independent Kosovo. Under pressure from KFOR and from Western governments, the KLA agreed to disband, but key elements survived in the form of a political party, headed by Thaci, and a 'Kosovo Protection Corps', under the former KLA commander, Agim Ceku. The latter clearly sees itself as the future army of a sovereign Kosovo state; tough negotiations with KFOR over the Corps' name and status did not diminish this aspiration. The former moved quickly to take power at the local level, partly through intimidation, partly because they were welcomed as heroes anyway, and partly because there was a power vacuum to be filled.

The complicity of the top KLA leadership in the killings of Serbs and other minorities is not entirely clear. Lines of responsibility are obscured by the loose structure of the KLA, always more 'an association of clans' than a tightly organised command structure.[5] Ethnic and political crimes are tangled up with the profit-seeking gangsterism of a wider Albanian mafia. Yet it would be naïve to suggest that the Albanian acts of revenge have been random or spontaneous. On the contrary, their logic is the logic of ethnic cleansing. Such ethno-nationalist extremism is consistent with political extremism against one's own ethnic kin, so it is perhaps not surprising that a series of political assassinations targeted officials of the KLA's main rival, Rugova's LDK. Finally, just as the KLA succeeded in making NATO their air force, after the war some armed guerrillas tried to use KFOR's buffer zone around Kosovo as a base for mounting raids into Albanian-populated territory of the Presevo Valley in Serbia proper. The apparent hope was to provoke Serb reprisals against Albanian villagers on such a scale that NATO would be forced, once again, to intervene on the side of the Albanians.[6]

The KLA problem looked slightly less daunting after local elections in October 2000 and parliamentary elections in December 2001 delivered convincing victories to Rugova's LDK. If the results did not constitute an outright rejection of armed militancy, they did tend to confirm an encouraging regional trend favouring (relatively) moderate alternatives. Together with the victories of opposition candidates in Yugoslavia and Croatia, the Kosovo elections supported hopes that the appeal of extreme nationalists throughout the region could be waning.

Kosovo independence?

Although they had fought a war on the side of Kosovar separatists, and had demanded the effective removal of Serb authority, the NATO powers afterwards did try to maintain the same principles of territorial integrity that they had espoused in the years leading up to the war. The international recognition of the former Yugoslavia's dissolution in 1992, carefully articulated in the findings of the

Badinter Commission, had been based on the international status of *republic* borders, a status acknowledged in Yugoslavia's constitution. *Ethnic* partition, on the other hand, was seen to have no logical conclusion, particularly in the Balkans. Accepting Kosovo's independence was seen as inconsistent with the interest in maintaining Macedonia's integrity, and the formal unity of Dayton Bosnia. Moreover, without questioning the Rugova leadership's impressive moral posture since 1989, there was reason to worry – even before KLA conduct became a concern – about whether a state created on the principle of *ethnic* self-determination would be a particularly democratic one, or particularly liberal in its treatment of minority Serbs who wished to remain. In any event, Moscow had endorsed UNSC Resolution 1244, which set out the terms for Belgrade's capitulation, only on the basis of language recognising Yugoslavia's territorial integrity.

In the first days of the bombing campaign, President Clinton had warned that a natural consequence of Belgrade's actions could be Serbia's loss of Kosovo. News reports in the late summer of 1999 suggested the possible beginnings of a transatlantic row, with US officials speaking off-the-record about the inevitability of independence and European officials reacting angrily to what they regarded as a breach of alliance understandings.[7] After the autumn 2000 Yugoslav and Kosovo elections, there was further European irritation at suggestions that in the American interpretation of UNSC 1244, full independence was not precluded. Yet this remained a somewhat abstract disagreement. Anti-Serb excesses had cost the Albanians much of their support in Washington, and US policy did not promote formal independence, which would, in the words of one senior White House official, create 'an instant failed state'.[8] Given the anarchic conditions there, the judgement was almost certainly correct. US policy-makers generally agreed with their European counterparts that there were more urgent concerns than final status.

The first was to recreate some semblance of order. The second was to organise physical security and a political role for Kosovo's remaining Serbs. At the end of the war, leaders of that community had pleaded for a plan of ethnically based 'cantonisation' as the only way to safeguard the Serb future there. The NATO powers, seeing in it a thinly veiled bid for partition, refused. It proved true, however, that the Serbs were not safe except in a handful of isolated and protected enclaves, and in larger numbers in the northern half of the divided city of Mitrovica.

A third concern was how to manage the politically necessary ambiguity about Kosovo's final status. NATO's greatest nightmare was that Kosovar Albanians would come to see KFOR as an occupying force, and organise another guerrilla resistance. To forestall that future, the West – even if constrained to avoid offering independence – also needed to avoid any steps that precluded the option. In this context, it is a mistake for Western officials to discuss the democratisation of Serbia as though it provides the answer to future relations between Serbs and Kosovars. After what they suffered at Serb hands, Albanians will be unwilling to submit even to the perfectly democratic domination of a Serb majority. The use itself of the word 'autonomy' is also unhelpful (albeit difficult to avoid, since it is contained in UNSC Resolution 1244). When they hear the word, Kosovars suspect an attempt to make them settle for the provincial autonomy they enjoyed under Yugoslavia's 1974 constitution. In rejecting that idea – and that of Kosovo as a third Yugoslav republic, mooted in the mid-1990s by some prominent Kosovars – they argue, firstly, that this autonomy was viable only within the federal balance of the larger Yugoslavia; and secondly, that autonomy would be worthless now, given how easily it was abolished.[9]

The first move toward real self-government came with the May 2001 promulgation – by then UNMIK head, Hans Haekkerup – of a 'Constitutional Framework for Provisional Self-Government in Kosovo'. Setting up a 120-seat parliament, with ten seats reserved for Kosovo Serbs and another 10 for other minorities, the framework respected the principles, but also the uneasy compromises contained in UNSC Resolution 1244.[10] UNMIK retains a veto over any acts of the assembly or government that are deemed to be at odds with 1244, such as a referendum or declaration of independence. It contains 1244's acknowledgement of Yugoslav sovereignty over Kosovo, but also hints of flexibility in interpreting that sovereignty – including the commitment that final status will be resolved in a way that takes account of the will of Kosovo's population.

Kosovo Serbs complained about the framework as a step towards independence; Albanians complained because it lacked a guarantee for an eventual referendum, or even a Rambouillet-style three-year deadline for addressing the final-status issue. Given the undimmed nationalism and enmity on both sides, the fact that both were unhappy with the framework could be deemed a good thing. But the test of this next stage of international administration will be to reassure both minority Serbs and majority Albanians that they are not at risk of being dominated by the other group. For Serbs, that is a nearly impossible challenge, but it should entail some form of substantial autonomy – 'functional' if not territorial.[11] For the Albanians, it should include every possible reassurance that – whatever their international 'status' may be – they will not have to submit again to Belgrade's rule.

Greater Albania?

Worries about Kosovo independence are usually linked to two knock-on effects. First, it is expected to lead almost inexorably to the break-up of Macedonia. Second, it is seen as a step toward a 'greater Albania' with claims to Kosovo, western Macedonia, parts of Montenegro and Serbia and even, in some scenarios, northern Greece.

These fears are overblown. The spectre of greater Albania tends to ignore not only the tremendous weakness of the Albanian state, but also the reality that this state has given little or no cause to be suspected of irredentism. It was Belgrade, not Tirana, that has promoted the idea that state authority must extend to incorporate all territories where ethnic kin live – an idea whose terrible consequences made victims of the Serbs along with everyone else. This is not to say, however, that concerns about potential Albanian irredentism are groundless. They derive from the unsettled status of an Albanian nation scattered among three states: some 3.4m in Albania itself (the poorest people in Europe by far); 1.8m in Kosovo (and still nominally part of Yugoslavia); 600,000 in Macedonia; plus another several hundred thousand in Serbia proper, Montenegro, Greece and Western Europe. Nowhere else in Europe does roughly half of a people with highly developed national consciousness live outside the borders of their putative nation-state, and in states where they have been despised, repressed and driven out by the Slav majority (Yugoslavia); or uneasily accommodated (Macedonia). The Albanian–Greek relationship – both cross-border and within Greece – is also full of resentment and ethnic antagonism.

A more concrete dimension of the 'Greater Albania' nightmare is criminal rather than political. The network of Albanian mafias running lucrative trade in drugs, guns and women darkens the reputation of an entire national group. In Macedonia, for example, the ethnic Macedonian majority look with great suspicion and resentment at the visible prosperity and astonishing construction boom in the Albanian-populated town of Gostivar. Such suspicions are undoubtedly fuelled by a large element of ethnic prejudice, while the organised-crime connections of some Albanian politicians hardly make them unique in the region. Yet, given the rampant criminality of economic life just over the border in Albania and Kosovo, the suspicions cannot be dismissed out of hand.

Against the threats of both political irredentism and criminal anarchy, the West needs to promote a stable Albanian state. A first attempt to do so had mixed results. The US–Albanian strategic relationship of the 1990s was partly discredited as the regime of then President Sali Berisha slid from authoritarian populism to authoritarian thuggery, and as the whole country slid into chaos after the financial meltdown of spring 1997. Critics charged that Berisha had been allowed to interpret American patronage as a superpower licence for his petty despotism. Yet, in return for its patronage, Washington was able to demand from Tirana a policy of moderation towards the Albanian populations of Kosovo and Macedonia. Given that Albanian irredentism did not gain momentum, US policy has to be judged a success. A continuing Western presence, including significant help with criminal law enforcement, is needed to reassure neighbouring countries that have real, albeit exaggerated, fears of a 'Greater Albania'.

Macedonia

From the early 1990s, as Yugoslavia suffered its wars of ethnic cleansing, there was much speculation about the consequences of Macedonia succumbing to the same fate. Some of the more alarming scenarios – such as a general south Balkans war drawing in Bulgaria, Greece and Turkey – never seemed very logical. The real challenges to Macedonian identity and stability – including nationalist hostility and a damaging blockade from EU- and NATO-member Greece – were grave enough. Skopje was compensated, however, with an intense degree of Western solicitude, including aid, advice and the 'preventive' UN deployment of 1,000 Scandinavian and US troops (America's first substantial Balkans deployment). The biggest test

Map 2 South Balkans: Ethnic Albanian Populations

Location	Total population	Albanian percentage
Albania	3,418,900	95%
Serbia (without Kosovo)	8,493,600	2%
Kosovo	1,900,000	90%
Montenegro	610,000	7%
Macedonia	2,159,500	23–33%
		(Albanians claim 40%)

Sources: Various. All figures, especially for Serbia and Kosovo, should be viewed as approximate. Based on a table in 'Greater Albania' by Tim Judah, *Survival*, vol. 43, no. 2, Summer 2001, p. 11.

was the Kosovo war itself. But, while Macedonia's government was alarmed and its Slavic majority enraged by the war, Skopje rapidly came to recognise its interest in an early NATO victory. Among other rewards, that victory meant the astonishingly rapid return of almost all Kosovar refugees. Their long-term presence could have had a devastating effect on the psychological balance of Macedonian ethnic relations.

In any event, for most of its first decade as an independent state, Macedonia confounded the pessimists by surviving. But starting in February 2001, armed ethnic conflict finally came to the country, and the pessimists had reason to feel vindicated. At first, officials in Skopje tried to suggest that the armed rebellion was entirely imported from Kosovo. This was wrong: Western journalists found a high degree of at least tacit support for the guerrillas from Macedonia's Albanians; and the fighters themselves include many Albanians from the Macedonian side of the border (a border that is of relatively recent salience anyway).

It is true enough, however, that Kosovar guerrillas crossed the border in search of a fight. Albanian–Slav tensions in Kosovo and in Macedonia are intimately linked, though the linkage does not operate in quite the straightforward manner than many assume. Macedonia's troubles came – not with an increasing prospect of Kosovo independence – but at a time when Kosovars feared that the prospect was fading. With Milosevic deposed in Belgrade, Western powers were more solicitous of the Yugoslav and Serb governments' views. And with a Republican administration replacing the Clinton administration in Washington, Albanians felt they were losing an important ally and patron.[12]

Like the emergence of the KLA in Kosovo, the National Liberation Army in Macedonia moved in the course of a few months from shadowy rumour to fierce gun-battles: skirmishing with Macedonian army and police in January and February 2001; battling for villages around Tetevo in April and May; and then advancing in June to the village of Aracinovo, just eight kilometres away and within shelling distance of the capital, Skopje. Counter-attacks by Macedonian security forces involved the worst possible combination of military incompetence and occasional brutality. There were burned-out villages reminiscent of Serb scorched-earth tactics in Kosovo; there were also allegations of low-level ethnic cleansing of both ethnic Macedonian and Albanian communities, and some 50,000 refugees. A full-scale civil war looked imminent.

But unlike Kosovo, the full-scale war was averted. In August, under relentless European and US pressure, Macedonia's ethnic Macedonian and Albanian politicians concluded, at Lake Ohrid near the Albanian border, a 'Framework Agreement' for cease-fire, disarmament of the rebels and constitutional and political reforms to secure Albanian rights. Four of these reforms were most important:

- Amending the preamble to the constitution to remove the statement that 'Macedonia is the state of Macedonians and its minorities'.
- The designation of Albanian as a second official language, which citizens can use in their dealings with authorities in any district where the Albanian population exceeds 20%.
- A hiring programme to ensure 'as rapidly as possible that the police services will generally reflect the composition and distribution of the population of Macedonia'.
- A programme of government decentralisation designed to give Albanian-dominated areas greater autonomy over culture, education, health-care and other public services.[13]

There were three reasons that this agreement could be reached. Firstly, Western diplomatic engagement to solve the crisis was swift, unified and coherent. European leaders moved quickly. Javier Solana, the EU's High Representative for Foreign Policy, and NATO Secretary-General George Robertson were almost constantly in Skopje, pressing leaders of both sides to settle. US support was highly visible, and increasingly so, as American diplomat James Pardew joined the EU's François Leotard in mediating the actual deal.

Secondly, Western engagement included a willingness to deploy 4,000 NATO troops to supervise the disarmament, and a follow-on force of roughly 1,000 to provide general reassurance to both sides and direct security to OSCE monitors of the Ohrid Agreement's implementation. This was critically important because NATO could provide the only security forces trusted by both sides (though the ethnic Macedonians were suspicious of what they considered a pro-Albanian bias). To be sure, NATO governments were politically unprepared for the prospect of a more serious force to actually confront the Albanian guerrillas and restrain the government forces. If such a robust intervention had proven necessary, NATO almost certainly would have conducted it, but may well have been too late. Happily, it did not prove necessary. And NATO deftly avoided the familiar transatlantic problem of the Americans and Europeans holding one another hostage to the other's wariness. The European side accepted early on that the US would provide only logistical support; Britain took command of the disarmament force and Germany of the follow-on force. The arrangement – in essence, an example of 'separable but not separate' capabilities envisioned, in the St Malo initiative, for a European operation under NATO flag – worked well.

Finally, it is fair to say that both sides feared the consequences of all-out war, and were prepared for compromises to avoid it. The Albanians' programme was not maximalist. This was true even of the NLA, which was not a direct party to the negotiations, but which was ready to lay down its arms – in at least symbolic numbers – in exchange for a reform package that the Macedonian government probably should have offered anyway. But the spirit of compromise was limited, and therein lies the continuing danger to Macedonia. The Albanian programme *was* full of nationalist emotion and symbolism; this included the mainstream Albanian politicians who were part of Macedonia's coalition government and who had condemned the violence. Too often, these politicians have put forward agendas that have more to do with nationalist symbolism than with practical measures to improve the lot of the minority. Thus, at various times in the past decade, ethnic relations have been strained by such Albanian rallying cries as demands for an Albanian-language university, the right to fly Albanian flags over municipal buildings or the recasting of Macedonia as a bi-national confederal state.

Moving from symbolism to concrete improvements in the minority's second-class status requires an effective state and good faith from ethnic Macedonian politicians. The former is lacking, while the latter cannot be taken for granted. After the August signing, the US and European mediators were furious at a move to make the ratification of the Ohrid package dependent on a nation-wide referendum, which would mean likely rejection by the polarised ethnic Macedonian majority. The ethnic Macedonians were furious because they felt that the Western allies had effectively rammed the Ohrid Agreement down their throats, in order to appease armed Albanian 'terrorism'. They were essentially right about this. Notwithstanding the first statement of 'basic principles' in the Ohrid text – that the 'use of violence in pursuit of political aims is rejected completely and unconditionally'[14] – it was in fact violence that made the text possible. The unhappy pattern in all former Yugoslav republics thus finally came to the last of them. This was lamentable, but the violence was so far limited, and alternative to Ohrid's implicit appeasement of it was – and may still be – a war that destroys Macedonia.

Serbia and Montenegro

In October 1998, as NATO first geared up for an air campaign against Serbia, some US officials were saying privately that if air strikes went forward, their only rational purpose would be to drive Milosevic from office.[15] As the war ended with him still in power, NATO leaders continued to hope that the man who had brought Serbia to such unparalleled disaster finally would have lost the confidence of his people and elites.

Milosevic had faced just that crisis in the aftermath of the Bosnian war, when a mass civic movement took to the streets daily for three months over the winter of 1996–97. He had defeated that challenge through a combination of minor concessions and the shrewd exploitation of divisions among opposition leaders (one of whom, Vuk Draskovic, eventually crossed over to join the govern-ment). Following his Kosovo defeat, Milosevic apparently was counting on similar opposition weakness and confusion when he called new Yugoslav presidential elections for September 2000. But this turned out to be a miscalculation on the same order as assuming that NATO would eventually back down over Kosovo.

Inspiring as it was, the Kostunica victory over Milosevic was only a start on solving Serbia's many problems. There were, however, two transatlantic problems that it neatly defused. Firstly, the question of whether sanctions against Serbia were ineffective or even counter-productive now became academic. (The residual possibility that Washington, and especially the US Congress, would insist on maintaining the 'outer wall' of international financial institution sanctions ended with Belgrade's delivery of Milosevic to The Hague.) Secondly, the significant danger of yet another war – this time between Serbia and Montenegro – again drawing NATO intervention had all but vanished. Montenegrins were always considered loyal cousins of the Serbs, but the tiny republic became a wild card in Yugoslav politics after Milo Djukanovic, a Milosevic opponent, narrowly won a bitter presidential election in October 1997. Milosevic's response was a refusal to seat the delegates of

Montenegro's elected parliament in the federal legislature. Two years later, a constitutional amendment effectively demolished any pretence of a federal system: deputies to the upper chamber were now to be elected directly, bypassing the Montenegrin parliament and thus eliminating tiny Montenegro's guaranteed presence of 20 seats. It was all of a pattern with the constitutional machinations of the late 1980s that led to the Balkan wars of the 1990s. The Kosovo war helped underscore the benefits of a pro-Western alignment, since Montenegrins were largely spared the NATO bombing. The result was a government strategy of 'creeping independence' that achieved the republic's *de facto* independence in every respect but one: the continued presence of the Yugoslav Army. All the while Djukanovic threatened to follow the examples of Slovenia, Croatia, Bosnia and Kosovo by holding a referendum on independence. But he acknowledged that Montenegro was deeply divided on the issue, and so continued to refrain from doing so.[16] The fear of military crackdown or a coup attempt became more intense as it became clear that Milosevic might actually lose his election, and start looking for a diversion.

With Milosevic out of power, the question of Montenegro's relationship with Serbia could be settled without violence. There were strong political pressures on the Montenegrin government – from within the governing coalition and among its electoral constituencies – to stay on course for independence. However, there was also strong pressure from the European Union against formal secession. EU governments were probably most concerned about the implications for Kosovo. If there was to be any future for Kosovo in Yugoslavia, it could only be on the basis of a triangular confederal relationship that included Montenegro. But that was a slim hope anyway, and independence-minded Montenegrins complained that they were being held hostage to a Western illusion.

Nonetheless, following heavy mediation by EU foreign-policy High Represenative Javier Solana, Kostunica and Djukanovic on 14 March 2002 signed an agreement turning the Yugoslav federation into a loose 'Union' of Serbia and Montenegro. The agreement maintains a common foreign and defence policy and a unitary international personality for the two republics. But it also preserves Montenegro's *de facto* separation on most domestic matters including currency, economic systems and customs. It also stipulates that Montenegro has the right, after three years, to opt out of the arrangement after all.

Post-war administrations

Even the most dramatic political changes in Croatia and Serbia cannot relieve Western powers of their responsibilities for the post-war administration of Bosnia and Kosovo. This involves the unavoidable but inherently controversial task of 'nation building'. Both territories have become Western protectorates in terms of NATO's strategic investment and local expectations about the Western role. Bosnia and Kosovo are not, however, legal protectorates in the classic sense; they are not cases of some single state or authority taking sovereign responsibility for managing a territory in transition to independence. Therein lies a great weakness of these efforts: in the diversity of institutions involved, the confusion of authority and the ambiguity about purpose.[17]

Timid enforcement and fractured authority

Part of the problem is philosophical. At Dayton, the Bosnian parties effectively submitted themselves to a military occupation. Yet the occupying powers were reluctant to behave as such. As discussed in Chapter 2, the American military was loath to become mired in 'nation-building' or 'mission-creep'. International administrators, steeped in democratic and anti-colonial traditions, were reluctant to execute their mandates too imperiously. The OHR promulgated a concept of 'ownership' under which Bosnian parties are supposed to take charge of their own peace-building. This concept was based on a serious underestimation of the purposeful obstructions, dysfunctional animosities and overall breakdown of Bosnian society. One unfortunate example was the conduct of the first post-Dayton elections of September 1996, which resulted in little more than an ethnic census-taking.[18] The traumas of an ethnic war were not likely to be overcome by an abrupt electoral reconciliation. To equate the mechanics of elections with democracy and ethnic reconciliation was part of the greater illusion that a quick and peaceful exit strategy was available.

The Bosnian peace-implementation effort also suffered from a crippling failure of coordination, not only between IFOR/SFOR and civilian implementers, but also among the civilian agencies. Local parties became masters at exploiting transatlantic divisions – 'shopping around for a better deal', in the words of one top OHR official.[19] In 1997, for example, the OHR tried to insist on the issuance of a truly common currency, the convertible mark, backed one-to-one by the deutschemark. But the US, driven by deadline pressures and determined to have a functioning currency, undercut the OHR's hard line by backing a compromise whereby the *Republika Srpska* was permitted to issue its own marks.[20] Similarly, in divided Mostar, site of some of the most bitter fighting between Croats and Muslims, EU administrator Hans Koschnik had for months made clear his intention to implement a redistricting that would unify the Muslim and Croat halves of the city. When he presented the detailed plan, however, his life was seriously threatened in a riot organised by the Croat mayor of West Mostar. Within weeks of this incident, the EU gave up on Koschnik's plan: Italy had just taken over the EU presidency; its Foreign Minister Susanna Agnelli was poorly briefed on the importance of the issue; and Germany, which had backed Koschnik, did not take a strong stand in apparent deference to the principle of rotating EU presidency.

The principle of conditionality was undermined by the reality of too many independent sources of reconstruction aid. If OHR tried to punish a municipality for non-compliance by withholding aid, another national donor would often barge in to offer the money.[21] Perhaps the most important tensions of this nature involved the World Bank, with a generally 'non-political' doctrine that often put it at odds with the OHR's very political agenda.

In Kosovo, some of these problems were avoided. UNMIK established much more of a real protectorate from the beginning, with more coherent lines of authority. The international presence was organised in a 'pillar system' under which organisations such as OSCE or UNHCR, while not always deferring to the Special Representative of the Secretary-General in Kosovo, initially Bernard Kouchner, made a clear effort to communicate with UNMIK and coordinate their activities. Most critically, KFOR has put itself at the service of UNMIK for a variety of 'nation-building' tasks. Compared to IFOR in Bosnia, there were far fewer objections to 'mission creep' from the commanders of international troops in Kosovo.

Law and order

One reason that KFOR was willing to accept a broader mandate is that conditions in Kosovo left it with no choice. Kosovo after its war was far more lawless than Bosnia after Dayton. The war had been too short – as one UNMIK official put it grimly – for hatreds to burn themselves out.[22] Moreover, the withdrawal of Serb forces and the absence of an Albanian police force left KFOR as the only agent that could establish any order whatsoever.

The experience did confirm some of the military misgivings about soldiers as police: there was at least one report of physical threats to extract confessions; and more frequent complaints about soldiers who were themselves clueless on basic procedures for collecting evidence. But there were also large differences between national contingents, which suggested that it is not impossible to train soldiers to be police. In Kosovo as in Bosnia, British troops generally received the highest marks for physically protecting minorities and aggressively confronting ethnic troublemakers. Their difficult experiences in Northern Ireland had evidently fed into a robust doctrine of peacekeeping. By the same token, US troops were criticised for being excessively concerned with force protection.

Efforts to import actual police to both Bosnia and Kosovo proved frustrating, though for different reasons in each case. In Bosnia, the international police were there purely for advisory and training purposes, and their commanders had concluded by the end of the decade that they should have had executive authority to actually investigate crimes and make arrests.[23] For Kosovo, the option of an international police force without 'executive' authorities was ruled out from the beginning as a luxury that the lawless territory could not afford. But the problem was numbers: Kouchner had asked for 6,000, was authorised to hire 4,000, and had trouble recruiting even at that level. By the summer of 2000, he had concluded that no more were coming, and that he would have to rely on the training of local police. UNMIK had some successes here, even in the recruitment of Serbs (though exclusively for the Serb enclaves). But establishing a professional police force was only part of the problem; for sensitive cases crossing ethnic lines, local judges were seen as hopelessly biased or easily subject to intimidation. Thus UNMIK faced the daunting challenge of recruiting a cadre of international judges as well.

Planning and staffing

Recruitment was arguably UNMIK's greatest failure. The UN system of filling posts on the basis of geographical diversity meant that many were not filled at all. One year after the war, the UNMIK staffing table was roughly 60% full, and the consequences of this shortfall were devastating. In the entire region of Prizren, for example, covering

Kosovo's second largest city and a large chunk of territory, there was, for more than six weeks after the war, one UN official. Under these circumstances, it was hardly surprising that the KLA members were able to take over much of the local administration, and neither UNMIK nor KFOR were in much position to object, since they could offer no practical alternatives.

The staffing shortfalls compounded the absence of early planning. UNMIK perhaps should not be blamed for this, since the UN's responsibility for the province was established only at the last minute, in a kind of sham concession to Belgrade and Moscow. Yet it does seem extraordinary that for more than two months of war, hardly anyone on the NATO side was making detailed plans for the consequences of victory.

Long-term strategies

The attempt to determine a long-term Western strategy for the Balkans as a whole was fraught with transatlantic tensions. These stemmed in part from the familiar and largely manageable question of transatlantic 'burden-sharing'. But there is also a risk of deeper misunderstandings. Washington sometimes seems to disregard the difficulties of an EU balancing act between constitutional deepening on the one hand and stabilising its periphery on the other. Similarly, European governments do not always seem to appreciate the tensions inherent to America's divided responsibilities as both a European and a global power.

These misunderstandings can be significantly damaging because they give rise to unintended signals affecting the psycho–logical dimension of Balkan security. The horrors that occurred during Yugoslavia's break-up in the 1990s make it impossible for survivors to ignore the possibility of their reoccurrence. This drives a familiar security dilemma – which, in its most extreme form, translates as 'dominate or be dominated', even to the point of 'kill or be killed'. Less extreme versions still tend to preclude the kind of ethnic tolerance that the West hopes to see established in the region. A withering of economic prospects, while not in the first instance causing the dilemma, deeply compounds it.

In principle, the Western strategy to relieve this insecurity is clear enough. Allaying physical and psychological insecurity requires the physical presence of NATO troops on a sufficiently permanent basis to dampen unsettling speculations about what will happen after they leave. Creating future prospects for something other than war requires the deployment of 'soft power' on a vast scale. In addition to material aid, this means fostering regional cooperation and a realistic, if very long-term prospect for admitting all of the Balkan states into the EU.

Confidence in the first pillar – military presence – was shaken in the 18 months following the Kosovo intervention by renewed uncertainty about US engagement. A number of members of the US Congress argued that US troops should withdraw unless the situation on the ground improved and/or the European allies took over more of the burden. During the 2000 US presidential campaign, candidate George W. Bush accused the Clinton administration of having damaged military 'readiness' through inadequate defence spending and too many overseas commitments, the Balkans deployments in particular. Bush's foreign-policy adviser (and later National Security Adviser), Condoleezza Rice, was more specific in a *New York Times* interview: there should be a new division of labour, she said, with the European allies concentrating on peace-keeping and the United States husbanding its resources for 'major-war' contingencies in East Asia and the Persian Gulf.[24] The discussion (one of the very few devoted to foreign policy in the presidential contest) underscored once again the ambivalence of the American military commitment to Kosovo and Bosnia. The prospect of an American withdrawal threatened to undermine the region's psychological security, as so clearly happened in Bosnia during the first 18 months of Dayton's implementation.[25]

Once in office, the new administration did what it could to dispel the uncertainty. Secretary of State Colin Powell promised that US troops would not withdraw ahead of the Europeans, and this commitment was soon endorsed by President Bush himself. In effect, the administration was accepting the argument that various Balkan protagonists, in particular the Serbs and Albanians, would be likely to exploit the inevitable transatlantic differences flowing from unequal American and European roles. Moreover, withdrawing US troops from the Balkans would raise the question of why they were needed in Europe at all. This might be a reasonable question, but is presumably not one that the new US administration was eager to raise.

US complaints about burden-sharing were not limited to military matters. The EU's reputation as an effective engine of soft power suffered greatly in late 1999, as the institution proved bureaucratically incapable of disbursing, in a timely fashion, the large sums of reconstruction aid it had promised. And its great post-war initiative, the Balkan 'Stability Pact', suffered for a long time from a lack of content and credibility. More important, perhaps, was the extent to which EU activities were couched in terms of the much larger project of EU enlargement to the East. Regional cooperation around Stability Pact projects, and so-called 'Stabilisation and Association Agreements' between the EU and various Balkan states, was supposed to become a kind of habit that would better prepare these countries for EU membership.

The link is not explicit, and many would deny that it exists at all (or makes any sense). This is a critical uncertainty, and a difficult obstacle to a coherent Western strategy for the region. On the one hand, the lure of EU membership constitutes a formidable source of Western leverage over Balkan states. And there is a certain geographical logic to their eventual EU integration. Slovenia, Romania and Bulgaria have been invited to begin accession negotiations, while Greece is already a member. There is a strong case for avoiding a scenario in which Croatia, Bosnia, Serbia, Montenegro, Kosovo, Albania and Macedonia would remain unstable enclaves, surrounded indefinitely by the European Union. On the other hand, it could be more than a generation before EU membership can seriously be discussed for most of them. Earlier membership for these countries might import conflict that would severely damage the effectiveness and cohesion of the EU, and would not do the Balkan states much good either.

Unfinished business

In all its planning for the Balkans, the alliance must be mindful of the implications for what can still be called 'Great Power' relations. In historical terms, those implications have been relatively benign. While the catastrophe of 1914 still casts a shadow, there was never a real danger of the Western powers being drawn in on opposite sides of Yugoslav conflicts in the 1990s. Much of the alarm about German support for Croatia amounted to a kind of historical shadow-boxing. Concerns about the spill-over effects on Greek–Turkish relations were more serious – though not in the sense sketched out in common scenarios of the Balkan conflict spreading to the Aegean. If Greece and Turkey were going to fight one another, they had plenty of disputes closer to home. The damage from the Yugoslav conflict was more insidious and, in a sense, cultural. Greece became embittered and significantly alienated from its NATO and EU partners because of popular support for Serbia, and because of the Greek nationalist reaction to the birth of a Macedonian state. In Turkey, Islamists seized on the plight of Bosnia as a potent symbol to discredit Ankara's Western alignments.[26]

Mujahideen from across the Arab and Islamic world came in the 1990s to fight in Bosnia and Kosovo. Some remained after the wars; the US 'Train and Equip' programme for Bosnia's Federation forces was held up by Washington until Sarajevo closed down training camps, expelled some of the Islamic fighters and dismissed the pro-Iranian defence minister. The Balkans are among the 'fields of jihad' proclaimed by Osama bin Laden; a cell of bin Laden operatives was expelled from Albania in 1999 before it could carry out an attack on the US embassy in Tirana. In October 2001, SFOR reported that its troops had rolled up a terrorist cell in Bosnia. It is fair to observe, with Marta Dassú and Nicholas Whyte, that the 'roots of Islamic fundamentalism in the Balkans are not particularly deep, and most Muslims in the region tend to be more pro-American than their Orthodox neighbours – hardly promising recruitment material for the al-Qaeda network'.[27] Still, the Balkan countries with large Muslim populations are all potential failed states. The nexus of organised crime throughout the region helps establish a kind of illicit infrastructure that can easily be exploited by terrorists. This (still latent) threat is another reason that NATO's military presence in the Balkans can be seen to serve direct strategic interests.

The most worrying spill-over effect concerns Western relations with Russia. Moscow seemed to be making a rational calculation of its broader interests and possibilities when it finally came round to supporting NATO's conditions for ending the Kosovo war. Still, Russians were furious about the NATO bombing campaign, and faced many temptations to play the spoiler. The race by a Russian unit from Bosnia to seize Pristina's airport before NATO's arrival was a modest indulgence of this temptation. Despite this, and despite the US determination to deny Russia its own peacekeeping zone, the

NATO powers remained anxious to keep up the fig leaf of Russian participation as a 'senior partner' in the management of the Kosovo protectorate, as a way to repair broader relations. Although Russian participation seemed at the time just as likely to be a source of serious friction on the ground (given Russian–American differences over final status, and given the Kosovar Albanians' bitter distrust of the Russians), there were no serious problems as of early 2002. Moscow's diplomatic attention to the Balkans has been uneven and inconsistent, and it has not invested so much prestige in a particular outcome that differences with the West need be irreconcilable.[28]

The apparent transformation, after 11 September, of Russia's relations with the United States and NATO should serve to de-emphasise disagreements concerning the Balkans. But it is equally true that progress and stability in the Balkans would ease the continued improvement of NATO–Russian relations.

Conclusion

Looking at the Balkans as a whole, it is difficult to deny the progress that has been made. Serbia's democratic government has acknowledged the crimes of its predecessor and is moving towards a Western alignment. Croatia has finally made credible commitments to respect the sovereignty of Dayton Bosnia, while significant refugee returns to Bosnia's minority areas have started. Greece is starting to assume a leadership role commensurate with its political and economic weight, and almost all the states of the region have demonstrated a new willingness to engage in regional cooperation as a platform towards European integration. And Macedonia – for the moment at least – has been pulled back from the brink of civil war. Such improvements, some modest but some quite dramatic, suggest that wartime hatreds and fanaticism will subside, given enough time and the right regional framework.

NATO governments can take some credit for imposing that framework, and it is within their power to sustain it. To do so, however, they need to remain broadly united about its shape. This is a lesson that Washington and its European allies evidently took to heart over the course of the 1990s: their Balkans 'learning curve' is discernible in the record of early failures and later success.

For the United States, preponderant power and prestige have gone together with a greater willingness to take sides in conflicts where it was sometimes difficult, but rarely impossible, to distinguish victim from aggressor. America was less willing, however, to engage in humanitarian interventions that risked the lives of its own soldiers or, indeed, to sustain a coherent long-term engagement of any kind. The Clinton administration gradually shed these inhibitions; and despite some remaining diffidence in parts of the new Bush administration, President Bush and Secretary of State Colin Powell soon came to acknowledge the necessity of an open-ended commitment of US troops. Yet this renewed commitment was undermined, almost immediately, by the new pressures on US foreign policy arising from the events of 11 September.

For America's European allies, the lesson has to be that the uncertainties of US commitment are not just a matter of government policy, but are inherent to American history, domestic politics and geostrategic responsibilities. The allies can continue to argue against a US withdrawal from Kosovo and Bosnia, for the sake of NATO solidarity as well as Balkan security. Yet rather than aggravating Balkan insecurities by holding their own troop presence hostage to the American deployment, they should make an unequivocal commitment to stay for as long as necessary. EU efforts since 1998 to develop an autonomous military capability are an important step towards making such a commitment credible. Failure, however, to match the EU 'headline goal' with adequate defence spending, rationalised procurement and real capabilities would raise the spectre of another hollow 'hour of Europe'. The Balkans – whatever progress has been made – remain sufficiently unstable and unpredictable to deliver another devastating blow to European credibility.

Hard choices: Macedonia, Kosovo and Bosnia

On such issues – the use of military force and transatlantic burden sharing – the allies have been able to achieve a rough consensus. Much more difficult is the problem of reconciling demands for national self-determination with the imperatives of stability and ethnic co-existence. This problem could take decades to 'solve'. For a start, therefore, policymakers on both sides of the Atlantic should avoid the temptation of couching their Balkan policies in inflated rhetoric. Unrealistic promises to create liberal multi-ethnic societies set up expectations that the missions are unlikely to meet. The consequent loss of support among Western publics can be very damaging. Such rhetorical over-reaching is unnecessary, for NATO did not intervene in the Balkans to create or even to preserve multi-ethnic states. Rather, NATO intervened, reluctantly and belatedly, to defeat the murderous ethnic cleansing that was integral to the project of a 'Greater Serbia'. With the Serb defeat in Kosovo, and earlier defeats in Croatia and Bosnia, a potentially terrible precedent has failed, and has been seen to fail.

To be sure, the interventions landed the NATO allies with the responsibility to establish conditions for long-term peace – and there is general (though not universal) agreement that this requires them to oppose the creation of mono-ethnic states. Sadly, however, mono-ethnic state formation continues. Croatia encouraged most of its Serbs to flee and, until Tudjman's death, it discouraged those who wanted to come back. Post-war Bosnia remains, in effect, three ethnic statelets united by a Western civil and military presence. Kosovo shows every sign of becoming another such statelet, nearly free of Serbs. Yet, although nationalist state formation is often linked to ethnic cleansing, it is not quite synonymous with it. The Western allies have the difficult task of reaching among themselves a viable, if largely implicit, understanding about where present borders and the principle of multi-ethnicity should be defended, and where they must be sacrificed. The most difficult cases are Macedonia, Kosovo and Bosnia.

Macedonia

Because Macedonia enjoyed peace throughout the 1990s, Western officials may have deceived themselves about the state of ethnic relations in the country. Those relations were bad, and the armed conflict of 2001 made them worse.

It should not be imagined that ratification of the Ohrid Agreement means that the crisis is over. Skopje is still not in a position – either politically or militarily – to solve its ethnic dilemmas on its own. Politically, the state is weak, and probably lacks the administrative elan to implement fully such important reforms as the creation of a multi-ethnic police force. Militarily, Macedonian security forces showed in the first half of 2001 that they were unable to quell the rebellion with methods acceptable to the West and, more importantly, to their own Albanian citizens. This is not to suggest that either Skopje or the Albanian rebels were operating in the same moral universe as Slobodan Milosevic's former regime. But moral chaos flowing from administrative incompetence can be bad enough. Resumed fighting with large-scale civilian deaths could push Macedonia's ethnic conflict past the point of amicable return. Another Kosovo comparison is worth bearing in mind: the Drenica massacre of early 1998 that turned a limited guerrilla campaign into a Kosovo-wide insurrection.

Even extraordinary (and unlikely) success in implementing the Ohrid Agreement would not necessarily solve Macedonia's security problem. Trouble might come again from across the border in Kosovo and, in any event, the calculations of guerrilla leaders concerning war and peace are opaque. While the insurrection clearly had some organic connection to the grievances of Macedonia's Albanians, it also has an autonomous life of its own, and thus a strictly political solution to it is not available. Insecurity breeds insecurity. If fighting resumes, NATO needs to be ready to enlarge substantially its small military presence as a supplement to, or even a substitute for, a political resolution. As in Bosnia and Kosovo, Western troops have come to be more or less trusted by both sides, and have been indispensable for post-conflict confidence and stability. The trust is far from absolute, and ethnic Macedonians have feared that NATO might establish *de facto* ethnic dividing lines, or a creeping protectorate that weakens rather than strengthening the Macedonian state. These fears are reasonable, but in the future they might have to be balanced against the prospect of a full-scale war that destroys the country and creates lasting enmity between its peoples.

The future of Kosovo

Kosovo has been separated, *de facto*, from Serbia. Recognition of its *de jure* separation will have to be delayed for several more years at a minimum: there is no consensus for it among the NATO allies, and Russia will remain adamantly opposed. Perhaps, after some years have passed, a formula might still be found under which the Kosovars would enjoy full self government but would also accept membership in a loose Yugoslav confederation. The chances are slim, however, and it would be a mistake to base Western policy on the illusion that even a fully democratised Serbia will ever again exercise effective sovereignty over Kosovo. Even with the best of will, no Serb leader can undo the fact that the Serb state recently drove the majority of Kosovars from their homes. Under these circumstances, the Clinton administration formulated the most realistic and sustainable policy, containing three elements:

- Firstly, Washington did not support Kosovo independence.
- Secondly, nor did the Americans rule it out.
- Thirdly, Kosovo's final status when it was decided should take into account the views of a majority of the territory's population.

The policy aimed at ambiguity, but it was hard to avoid the conclusion that ambiguity led in one direction only: independence. European governments, aware of the implications, objected. The George W. Bush administration, in line with its general de-emphasis of Balkan issues, seemed more inclined to defer to European sensitivities about Kosovo's future status. This was partly the consequence of a new administration not yet having set a clear policy, but the readiness to follow a European lead could only be reinforced by Washington's focus, post-11 September, on an overriding threat that had little to do with the Balkans.

Unity in favour of a misguided policy, however, can be worse than open disagreement. The unity is likely to last until the agreed opposition to independence proves untenable. Under the current difficult circumstances, even if independence remains politically and diplomatically unpalatable, the Western allies and the UN administration should promote Kosovo's more-or-less explicit 'Taiwanisation'. This means, in Veton Surroi's useful formulation, progressively to grant its majority population the prerogatives of 'statehood' if not 'sovereignty': building democratic institutions and imposing serious conditions on the Albanians' step-by-step assumption of self-rule.[1]

The most urgent of these conditions is the protection of Kosovo's Serbs and other minorities: both the physical security of the few who remain; and the legal rights of those who have fled but wish to return. On this matter the allies cannot afford to compromise. Not only would the emergence of a Serb-free Kosovo constitute a moral defeat; in political terms it would be an entity that NATO govern-ments would find difficult, over the long run, to defend with military force. And without NATO's military forces in Kosovo, Serb *revanchism* and Albanian extremism might one day produce another war.

It may be difficult to link the recognition of an independent Kosovo to its treatment of Serbs, for a somewhat paradoxical combination of reasons: on the one hand, some European governments refuse to concede that independence is even an option; on the other hand, it is hard to impose conditions on an outcome that looks inevitable anyway. Still, the West can emphasise one source of leverage that looks credible indeed, because it reflects facts on the ground. The ethnically compact area of Mitrovica, home to more than half of the territory's remaining Serbs, will be difficult in the best of circumstances to integrate into an Albanian-ruled Kosovo. Thoughtful Albanians know that their leadership has to offer the Serbs some plausible degree of autonomy.[2] Some Western experts have suggested that Mitrovica might attain a status comparable to *Republika Srpska* in Bosnia. In any event, UNMIK and the NATO governments can insist that there will be a Serb presence in the future Kosovo: in a multi-ethnic state, if the Albanians can organise one; or in a partitioned Kosovo, if they cannot.

The future of Bosnia

Bosnia's situation is different. The regime of President Alia Izetbegovic made a serious if imperfect effort – both during the war and afterwards – to maintain the kind of Bosnia and Herzegovina in which there would be a place for Serbs and Croats. And in 2000 the Itzetbegovic regime was replaced by a genuinely non-nationalist coalition. It may be that Dayton Bosnia has remained peaceful because the existence of *Republika Srpska* gives the Serbs such a high degree of autonomy. This pragmatic concession does not mean, however, that an entity created through ethnic cleansing should be rewarded with full independence. Bosnia's formal partition would require as much international policing as Dayton Bosnia, and at a greater cost in surrendered principles. If *Republika Srpska* were recognised as an independent state, or annexed to Serbia, the Bosnian Croats would demand the same. But the segregation of Croats and Muslims is not yet finished, particularly in central Bosnia, and its completion would involve more violence. Getting all sides to agree on the lines of partition would be nearly impossible: Muslims, when they have considered the idea of partition, have had in mind a Bosnian Muslim state that would include much of the present *Republika Srpska*. If it did not – if it corresponded merely to the Muslim controlled areas after Dayton – the result would be a 'rump' Bosnia, economically unviable and vulnerable to Muslim authoritarian currents. Unlike the Serbs and Croats, the Muslims do not have a neighbouring nation-state to which they can adhere. While the myth of a fundamentalist Bosnia was largely invented by its enemies' propaganda, a nationalist and authoritarian Bosnian Islam cannot be excluded in the future. And, of course, this rump Bosnia would contain several hundred thousand embittered refugees, looking across the borders to their lost homes, agitating to get them back. Such a future carries dangers of terrorism, shrill and undemocratic politics, regional instability and resumed war. It is a grim prospect, worth considerable effort to avoid.

The point here is not to argue that NATO powers must be prepared to compel the Bosnians to live together in a single state forever. Although the break-up of states is usually deplorable, it cannot always be avoided. There is such a thing as a velvet divorce: if Canada or Belgium were to split apart, the consequences would be unfortunate but manageable. Yet the obvious saving grace, in the hypothetical cases of Flemish or Quebecois secession, is that these separations would occur in a benign regional and international context. In the case of Bosnia, there cannot be – by definition – a 'velvet divorce' so close to a war of ethnic cleansing. In essence, the international community should enforce Dayton long enough for the Bosnian people to acquire some real choices that are not the direct consequences of that ethnic cleansing. Over time, other forces can take over. If their rights are enforced, refugees can return, gradually, even to minority areas. Greater links of commerce and journalism will develop between Banja Luka and Sarajevo, but also between Banja Luka and Zagreb – natural poles of attraction for reasons of geography and infrastructure. The passing from the scene of Franjo Tudjman and Slobodan Milosevic should help, as will democratisation and economic development. Time can cure much – it can be allowed to 'deconstruct', as Christopher Cviic has put it, the sharper edges of Dayton Bosnia. This might one day involve different political maps: such as the adherence of eastern *Republika Srpska* to Serbia, and of Banja Luka to a more unified Bosnia.[3]

For years to come, however, any reopening of Dayton would open a Pandora's box of new ethnic demands. Analysts might allude to alternative futures, but it is probably unwise for Western officials to concede too much. Continued commitment to Dayton is not so much a sign of dogmatism or limited imagination, but rather a determination to stick to the imperfect but existing set of principles around which the Western powers have a chance of staying united.

Are these arrangements – a protectorate leading to independence for Kosovo; another protectorate imposing formal unity on Bosnia – contradictory? Certainly there is some tension between them. Kosovo independence could very well be cited as a precedent by Serb secessionists in *Republika Srpska*, Croat secessionists in western Herzegovina and Albanian secessionists in Macedonia. All of these concerns underscore why the West is right to insist on maintaining recognised borders wherever it is realistic to do so. But it is not realistic to insist on Kosovo remaining part of Serbia. In the final analysis, moreover, there is a critical distinction between secession or partition, on the one hand, and ethnic cleansing, on the other. The former usually entails tragedy, but the latter is always a crime against humanity, and often a threat to international order.

Interpreting NATO's Balkan interventions

It was against this crime and this threat that the Western alliance twice intervened, the only occasions in its history that NATO as such has used military force. Expectations were raised of a new doctrine of humanitarian intervention. The 1990s were certainly the decade of enlarged consensus about the justification for such interventions, and there may even have been a certain ratcheting-up of readiness to undertake them.

The 11 September attacks on America, followed a month later by US–UK military action against Afghanistan, have arguably ushered in a different age of 'hyper intervention'.[4] The guiding principles of those interventions will almost certainly be closer to the wars of national survival – as in the Second World War – than to the 'wars of choice' to which Western publics have more recently been accustomed. 'Realist' aims have again become paramount: the set of Western policies falling under the rubric of a human-rights agenda cannot have the same priority that it did before September 2001. And yet, it may be that mobilisation on this scale, although its first aim is self-defence, will galvanise the Western allies to a more activist concern for misery across the globe. That is what happened to US foreign policy in the aftermath of the Second World War, and British Prime Minister Blair has argued forcefully that the anti-terrorism coalition should tie itself to post-war purposes of an equally ambitious scope. Certainly there seems to be an appreciation that post-war Afghanistan cannot again be left to its own devices.

At a moment of dramatic historical discontinuity, the interpretation of recent policies – and extrapolation into the future – demands a greater-than-usual degree of intellectual modesty. NATO's Balkan interventions may look, from this strangely distant strategic vantage point, like indulgences of a less demanding age. Yet those interventions were not undertaken lightly, and they were more than optional expressions of a humanitarian impulse. NATO employed military force in the Balkans only when moral imperatives were reinforced by a compelling interest in European stability. In today's more demanding strategic circumstances, maintaining that stability will be no small achievement.

Notes

Acknowledgements

For their advice and comments on earlier drafts, I would like to thank Gilles Andréani, Mark Baskin, Sidney Bearman, Christopher Bennett, David Calleo, Richard Caplan, Philip Gordon, Adam Roberts, John Roper, Jacques Rupnik, Jane Sharp, Steven Simon, Jonathan Stevenson, James Thomas, Mark Thompson and David Yost. In addition, Ann Danielson, Helga Haack, Daniel Halton and Genevieve Lester provided invaluable research assistance, while the Paul Nitze School of Advanced International Studies, The Johns Hopkins University, provided a home for an earlier stage of research. Finally, for her patience, special thanks to my daughter Sophie.

Introduction

[1] There is no satisfactory way of categorising the 'Muslim' nationality in Bosnia. To call them 'Muslims' suggests a more pronounced religious identity than is often present. In any event, if this group is 'Muslim,' why not label the Serbs 'Orthodox' and the Croats 'Catholics'? On the other hand, describing the Muslims as 'Bosniacs' – from the Serbo-Croatian 'Bosnjak' – might be taken to imply that they are the 'authentic' inhabitants of Bosnia. For lack of a better alternative, this paper uses 'Muslims' not in a religious sense but to denote the Muslim 'nationality' that was one of the officially recognised constituent nationalities of former Yugoslavia.

[2] Hans Morgenthau, 'Paradoxes of Nationalism', *Yale Review*, June 1957, p. 485.

[3] Leo Tindemans *et al.*, *Unfinished Peace: Report of the International Commission on the Balkans* (Washington DC: Carnegie Endowment for International Peace, 1996), p. 32. The present author served as Deputy Director of this commission.

Chapter 1

1 Lawrence Freedman, *The Revolution in Strategic Affairs*, Adelphi Paper 318 (Oxford: Oxford University Press for the IISS, April 1998), pp. 34–35.

2 See Adam Roberts, 'Communal Conflict as a Challenge to International Organization', in Alex Danchev and Thomas Halverson (eds), *International Perspectives on the Yugoslav Conflict* (New York: St. Martin's Press, 1996), p. 177.

3 Vance and Owen represented the United Nations and the European Union respectively as co-chairs of the International Conference on the Former Yugoslavia.

4 The US policies that were congruent with the policies of most European allies could be summarised in three phrases: not to intervene; to use diplomacy to support Yugoslav integrity and therefore little else; and to keep NATO out of it.

5 For a good analysis of the political currents against which Gulf War victory was of little help to Bush, see David Halberstam, *War in a Time of Peace: Bush, Clinton and the Generals* (New York: Scribner, 2001), pp. 9–156.

6 At the outset of Slovenia's short war of independence, in one of the more embarrassing flights of European *hubris*, Luxembourg Foreign Minister Jacques Poos proclaimed that it 'was the hour of Europe' and that 'if one problem can be solved by the Europeans, it's the Yugoslav problem. This is a European problem and it's not up to the Americans and not up to anybody else'. Jacques Poos on the ITN News, 28 June 1991, as cited in James Gow, *Triumph of the Lack of Will* (New York: Columbia University Press, 1997), p. 48. European Commission President Jacques Delors went so far as to warn in the summer of 1991 that an active American engagement would be regarded as meddling in European affairs: 'We do not interfere in American affairs; we hope they will have enough respect not to interfere in ours', as cited in *The Sunday Telegraph*, 16 May 1993.

7 One detects an element of *Schadenfreude* in the Bush administration's decision to let the Europeans try their hand at the crisis. John Newhouse, a leading chronicler of Western diplomacy, has even suggested a more calculated motive: by allowing the Europeans to take a test they were likely to fail, the issue of American leadership in NATO could be settled once and for all. John Newhouse, 'The Diplomatic Round: Dodging the Problem', *The New Yorker*, 24 August 1992.

8 See Russell Watson, 'Ethnic Cleansing', *Newsweek*, 17 August 1993, p. 16; Michael R. Gordon, 'Bush Backs a Ban on Combat Flights in Bosnia Airspace', *New York Times*, 2 October 1992, Section A, p. 1.

9 Michael R. Gordon, 'Powell Delivers a Resounding No on Using Limited Force in Bosnia', *The New York Times*, 28 September 1992, p. A1; and General Colin Powell, 'Why Generals Get Nervous', *The New York Times*, 8 October 1992, p. A35.

10 Cited in David Rieff, *Slaughterhouse: Bosnia and the*

Failure of the West (London: Vintage, 1995), p. 29.

[11] Arthur M. Schlesinger Jr., 'How to Think About Bosnia', *The Wall Street Journal*, 3 May 1993, p. A16.

[12] Brian Urquhart, 'Mission Impossible', *The New York Review of Books*, 18 November 1999, pp. 26–29.

[13] William Pfaff, 'Is Liberal Internationalism Dead?', *World Policy Journal*, vol. 10, no. 3, Fall 1993, p. 5.

[14] The concept of 'soft power' was used by Joseph Nye in *Bound to Lead: The Changing Nature of American Power* (New York: Basic Books, 1990). The debate continues, of course, about whether 'soft' or 'hard' power was most decisive in the West's victory. Both were obviously important. For the author's own extended contribution to this debate, see Dana H. Allin, *Cold War Illusions: America, Europe and Soviet Power, 1969–1989*, (New York: St. Martin's Press, 1994).

[15] Laura Silber and Allan Little, *The Death of Yugoslavia* (London: Penguin, 1995), p. 175.

[16] 'Genscher will einheitliche EG-Politik: Die Frage der Anerkennung Sloveniens und Kroatiens', *Frankfurter Allgemeine Zeitung*, 5 July 1991. See also Warren Zimmermann, *Origins of a Catastrophe: Yugoslavia and its Destroyers – America's Last Ambassador Tells What Happened and Why* (New York: Times Books, 1996), p.177.

[17] Anatol Lieven, 'The Weakness of Russian Nationalism', *Survival*, vol. 41, no. 2, Summer 1999, pp. 53–70.

[18] This time, the United States was a leading proponent of recognition, a position that was consistent, but not well-considered. In part, it was the poisonous effect of Croatia's recognition on EU and transatlantic relations that rendered rational discussion of the Bosnia case difficult.

[19] See Gilles Andréani, *Europe's Uncertain Identity* (London: Centre for European Reform, 1999), p. 26.

[20] David Rieff, *Slaughterhouse*; Diane F. Orentlicher, 'Genocide', in Roy Gutman and David Rieff (eds), *Crimes of War: What the Public Should Know* (New York: W.W. Norton & Co., 1999), pp. 153–157. See also Fouad Ajami, 'Under Western Eyes: The Fate of Bosnia', *Survival*, vol. 41, no. 2, Summer 1999, pp. 35–52.

[21] 'In the present Convention, genocide means any of the following acts committed with intent to destroy, in whole or in part, a national, ethnical, racial or religious group, as such: (a) Killing members of the group; (b) Causing serious bodily or mental harm to members of the group; (c) Deliberately inflicting on the group conditions of life calculated to bring about its physical destruction in whole or in part; (d) Imposing measures intended to prevent births within the group; (e) Forcibly transferring children of the group to another group'. Article 2 of *The United Nations Convention on the Prevention and Punishment of the Crime of Genocide*, approved and proposed for signature and accession by General Assembly Resolution 260 (III) A of 9 December 1948.

[22] Ronald Steel, *Temptations of a Superpower: America's Foreign Policy After the Cold War*

(Cambridge Massachusetts: Harvard University Press, 1995), p. 130.

23 Prosecutor *v.* Radislav Krstic Judgment (2 August 2001) pp. 188–212, specifically paragraphs 594–599, http://www.un.org/icty/krstic/TrialC1/judgement/krs-tj010802e.pdf.

24 See CBS News/New York Times Poll, 25 July 1995 and Times Mirror/Princeton Survey Research Associates Poll, 15 September, 1993; also, Richard Sobel, Chapter 6 in *US and European Attitudes Toward Intervention in the Former Yugoslavia: Mourir pour la Bosnie* (New York: Council on Foreign Relations, 1998).

25 See, for example, the complaints of the former US ambassador to Yugoslavia, Warren Zimmermann, *Origins of a Catastrophe*, p. 224.

26 See General Sir Michael Rose, *Fighting For Peace: Bosnia 1994*, (London: The Harvill Press, 1998).

27 David Owen, *Balkan Odyssey* (New York: Harcourt Brace, 1995), p. 199.

28 Zimmermann, *Origins of a Catastrophe*, p. 178.

29 Author/ICOB interview with President Franjo Tudjman, Zagreb, April 1996. This interview was one of a series that the author conducted in 1995–96 as part of a delegation from the Aspen-Carnegie International Commission on the Balkans (ICOB). Hereafter, these will be cited as 'author/ICOB interview' or, for meetings in which the author did not participate, simply 'ICOB interview'.

30 *Ibid.*

31 The referendum of 29 February and 1 March 1992 resulted in 63% of Bosnians voting for independence. The referendum was largely boycotted by Serbs. http://www.atlapedia.com/online/countries/bosnia.htm

32 See, for example, 'Report of the Secretary General pursuant to General Assembly resolution 53/35: The fall of Srebrenica', (New York: United Nations, 15 November 1999), paras 45–52, 57, 494–497.

33 Elizabeth Drew, *On the Edge: The Clinton Presidency* (New York: Simon & Schuster, 1994), pp. 155–158.

34 As former US Under Secretary of Defence (and later Deputy Defense Secretary) Paul Wolfowitz put it, since the bedrock 'of US policy under Bush and Clinton has been to keep US troops out', the only way to do so and still help the Bosnians would be to redress the Serbs' large tank advantage. Author/ICOB interview, Washington DC, February 1996.

35 Wolfowitz argued, for example, that the arms embargo on Spain during the civil war had delivered it to Hitler's designs. Weapons-supply programmes, on the other hand, he cited as powerful foreign-policy tools, e.g., Washington's Second World War lend-lease programme and US military aid to the Afghan rebels. *Ibid.* The historical pattern of arms embargoes penalising the weaker state or victims of aggression is discussed by Manfred Jonas, *Isolationism in America 1935–1941* (Ithaca, NY: Cornell University Press, 1966), pp. 172–173; and Henry Kissinger, *Diplomacy* (New York: Simon & Schuster, 1994), p. 385.

36 Whether the outrage was entirely ingenuous might be questioned.

37 Author interview with Peter Galbraith, Washington DC, 26 October 1999. See also Galbraith's testimony before the House International Relations Committee (30 May 1996). http://www.fas.org/congress/1996_hr/h960530ag.htm

38 Tindemans, *Unfinished Peace*, p. 75.

39 *Report of the Secretary-General Pursuant to General Assembly Resolution 53/35 (1998): 'Srebrenica Report'*, paragraphs 465–506.

40 Rieff, *Slaughterhouse*, p. 182. Owen was on record as having called for NATO to defend Bosnia with air strikes against the Serbs; see his open letter of 30 July 1992 to Prime Minister John Major, published in the *Evening Standard* and reprinted in *Balkan Odyssey*, pp.14–16.

41 Warren Zimmermann, *Origins of a Catastrophe*, p. 158. See also Carl Bildt, 'Force and Diplomacy', *Survival*, vol. 42, no.1, Spring 2000, p.142; and Owen, *Balkan Odyssey*, p. 12.

42 See, for example, the commentary by former UK diplomat Jonathan Clarke, 'Rhetoric Before Reality', *Foreign Affairs 74*, no. 5, September/October 1995, pp. 2–7.

43 The Contact Group included, at the time, the US, UK, France, Germany and Russia. For an analysis of the various plans, See Tindemans, *Unfinished Peace*, pp. 42–54.

44 For a balanced assessment of this charge, see Silber and Little, *Yugoslavia: Death of a Nation*, p. 297.

45 Vance and Owen insist that their plan preserved more Bosnian sovereignty, and was less of a blueprint for partition than Dayton. Several months after Dayton, Vance and his long-time deputy, Herbert Okun, listed four essential Serb war aims in Bosnia: a contiguous Serb state along the Drina; an ethnically cleansed state; the possibility for this state to join Serbia proper; and if there were to be a residual all-Bosnian government, that it should have no real powers. 'Vance-Owen explicitly rejected all four', claimed Okun. It was not based on ethnic division – of 10 proposed cantons, five had no ethnic majority. Serb majority cantons under the plan were not contiguous. Muslim enclaves that were later declared UN safe areas would have been in Muslim-controlled areas. (Under Dayton all except Gorazde are in the Srpska Republika.) Furthermore, a guaranteed right of refugee return would have mitigated against ethnic cleansing. Finally, said Okun, Vance-Owen explicitly rejected the notion of a 'special relationship' between Bosnian Serbs and Serbia proper. 'Now look at Dayton', he argued. 'It gives [Bosnia's Serbs] continuity [subject to the final disposition of Brcko]. It allows the special relationship. It speaks of refugee return or compensation, implying a greater degree of acceptance of ethnic cleansing. And regarding the powers of the central government, Okun complained, 'all three sides have a veto ... It is designed to be non-functional.' Author/ICOB interview with Cyrus Vance and Herbert Okun, New York,

February 1995. For a sympathetic commentary, see Michael Ignatieff, 'The Missed Chance in Bosnia', *"The New York Review of Books,* 29 February 1996.

46 Owen, *Balkan Odyssey*.

47 See for example, Anthony Lewis, 'Beware of Munich', *The New York Times*, 8 January 1993, p. A25; Anthony Lewis, 'The Clinton Doctrine?', *The New York Times*, 22 January 1993, p. A25; and Bruce W. Nelan, 'Serbia's Spite', *Time*, 25 January 1993, p. 48. The latter article commented, in a sub-headline: 'Milosevic should be pleased. If the West's peace plan goes into effect, it will ratify his aggression and grant him everything he wants'. Owen was convinced that such 'ill-informed attack[s]' in the American press hardened the Clinton administration against a meaningful endorsement. See Owen, *Balkan Odyssey*, pp. 100–101.

48 Vance himself later complained: 'The American government was not prepared to take the steps to let Vance-Owen live and breathe'. Author/ICOB interview.

49 Carl Bildt, 'Force and Diplomacy', *Survival*, vol. 42, no. 1, Spring 2000, p. 144.

50 Owen, *Balkan Odyssey*, p. 166.

51 David Rieff gives a good account of these false hopes and their insidious effect in *Slaughterhouse: Bosnia and the Failure of the West*, especially pp. 144–145.

52 Owen, *Balkan Odyssey*, p. 109.

53 See *Strategic Survey 1995/96* (London: Oxford University Press for IISS, 1996), p. 132.

54 Author interview, Peter Galbraith, Washington DC, October 1999.

55 Richard Holbrooke, *To End a War* (New York: The Modern Library, 1998), p. 64.

Chapter 2

1 Cited in William Drozdiak, 'Europe's Dallying Amid Crises Scares Its Critics', *International Herald Tribune*, 8 February 1996.

2 Harold Nicolson, *Peacemaking 1919* (London: Methuen & Co, 1964), p. 191.

3 Thus Baker's successor, Warren Christopher, explained in May 1993 why the United States would not send troops to protect the UN-proclaimed 'safe areas' of Sarajevo, Tuzla, Zepa, Gorazde, Bihac and Srebrenica. 'At heart', said Christopher, 'this is a European problem'. Warren Christopher, as quoted in Elizabeth Drew, *On the Edge*, p. 162.

4 Mark Danner, 'The US and the Yugoslav Catastrophe', *The New York Review of Books*, 20 November 1997, p. 58.

5 On the evolution and ramifications of the plan, see Ivo H. Daalder, *Getting to Dayton: The Making of America's Bosnia Policy* (Washington DC: Brookings Institution Press, 2000), *passim*.

6 Henry Kissinger, 'Limits to What the US Can Do in Bosnia', *Washington Post*, 22 September 1997, p. A19.

7 On the notion of a 'Grand Bargain', see Ronald D. Asmus, Robert D. Blackwill and F. Stephen Larrabee, 'Can NATO Survive?', *Washington Quarterly*, vol. 19, no. 2, 1996, pp. 79–101.

8 Martin Sieff, 'Iraq a Friction Point in Ties Among Allies', *Washington Times*, 15 February 1998, p. A10.

9. Quoted in Michael Dobbs, 'Holbrooke's Parting Shot – For Now', *Washington Post*, 3 March 1996, C1.

10. Ronald Steel, *Temptations of a Superpower* (Cambridge, MA: Harvard University Press, 1995), p. 80.

11. *Declaration on European Defence*, UK–French Summit, St Malo, 3–4 December 1998.

12. Author/ICOB interview with Wolfgang Ischinger, Bonn, 28 February 1996.

13. See for example, Carl Bildt, 'Force and Diplomacy', *Survival*, vol. 42, no. 1, Spring 2000, p. 144, and author/ICOB interview with Herbert Okun.

14. Michael C. Williams, 'The Folly of Partition', *Survival*, vol. 40, no. 2, Summer 1998, p. 183. Koljevic and then *Republika Srpska* Assembly President Momcilo Krajisnik made similar statements in this author's presence; author/ICOB interview, Pale, April 1996.

15. See *A Peace, or just a Cease Fire? The Military Question in post-Dayton Bosnia and Herzegovina*, International Crisis Group Report, 15 December 1997, Sarajevo, p. 18.

16. Author/ICOB interview with Herbert Okun; Christopher Bennett, 'The Bosnia Question', in Ben Reilly and Peter Harris (eds), *International Democracy and Deep-Rooted Conflict: Options for Negotiators*, Handbook Series 3 (Stockholm: International Idea, 1998).

17. Michael Dobbs, 'Despite Risks, Intervention Boosts Clinton', *Washington Post*, 14 October 1996, p. A1.

18. Author/ICOB interviews, Sarajevo, April 1996. See also Jane M. O. Sharp, 'Dayton Report Card', *International Security*, vol. 22, no. 3 Winter 1997/98, pp. 118–119.

19. Author interviews, Sarajevo, July 2000.

20. One notorious report had Karadzic himself passing easily through four IFOR checkpoints – including two American ones – on a trip from Pale to Banja Luka. John Pomfret, 'Bosnian Serbs' Leader Stages Show of Defiance', *Washington Post*, 10 February 1996.

21. Author/ICOB interviews with IFOR commanders, Sarajevo, April 1996.

22. For an example of this argument, see Anthony Lake, 'Defining Missions: Setting Deadlines: Meeting New Security Challenges in the Post-Cold War World,' speech at George Washington University, 6 March 1996, http://www.whitehouse.gov/WH/EOP/NSC/htm/nschome.htm#.speeches

23. 'The change was dramatic – 180 degrees – and we could see it on the very day that Clinton made the announcement', said one SFOR officer. Author interview with officer of northern command, Camp Eagle, Tuzla, 1998.

24. 'Chop Up Bosnia?', *The Economist*, 19 April 1997

25. Author interviews with OHR officials, Sarajevo, May 2000.

26. This insight was suggested to me by a European legal scholar attached to the OHR; author interview, Sarajevo, May 2000.

Chapter 3

1. For an early critique of NATO's air war, see Michael Mandelbaum, 'A Perfect Failure',

Foreign Affairs, vol. 78, no. 5, September/October 1999. For arguments that NATO should have intervened pre-emptively in 1992, see Zimmermann, *Origins of a Catastrophe*, pp. xi-xii, and Carl Bildt, 'Force and Diplomacy', p. 142.

2 Holbrooke, *To End a War*, p. 70; ICOB interview with Slobodan Milosevic, Belgrade, January 1996.

3 Mandelbaum, 'A Perfect Failure', p. 8.

4 David Binder, 'Bush Warns Serbs Not To Widen War', *New York Times*, 28 December 1992, p. A6.

5 Author interviews, Pristina, January 1996.

6 Steven L. Burg, 'Supporting Material,' in Barnett R. Rubin (ed.), *Toward Comprehensive Peace in Southeast Europe: Report of the South Balkans Working Group* (New York: the Council on Foreign Relations and the Twentieth Century Fund, 1996), pp. 30–33.

7 Mark Thompson, *Forging War: The media in Serbia, Croatia, Bosnia and Hercegovina* (Luton: University of Luton Press, 1999), pp. 51–107.

8 ICOB interview with Slobodan Milosevic, Belgrade, January 1996.

9 Author/ICOB interviews, Pristina, January 1996.

10 Tim Judah, 'Kosovo's Road to War', *Survival*, vol. 41. no. 2, Summer 1999, p. 13.

11 American pressure on Rugova to begin unconditional negotiations proved counter-productive: one May meeting, which could only take place if the LDK dropped its demand for international mediation, was followed within a week by a Serb offensive that drove some 20,000 refugees into the mountains of northern Albania.

12 See *Kosovo/Kosova: As Seen, As Told: An Analysis of the Human Rights Findings of the OSCE Kosovo Verification Mission*, October 1998 to June 1999, pp. 90–92.

13 Tim Judah, 'Kosovo's Road to War', p. 15.

14 A superb account of the Rambouillet talks is contained in Tim Judah, *Kosovo: War and Revenge* (New Haven: Yale University Press, 2000), pp.197–226.

15 As Veton Surroi, a Pristina newspaper editor and key member of the Kosovar delegation, interpreted it. Conversation with author, Budapest, March 1999.

16 Rambouillet Accord, 'Interim Agreement for Peace and Self-Government in Kosovo', 23 February 1999, Article I, paragraph 3. See: http://www.balkanaction.org.

17 *Ibid*, Article II, paragraphs 7–8.

18 Veton Surroi, conversation with author.

19 Rambouillet Accord, 'Interim Agreement for Peace and Self-Government in Kosovo', Appendix B: Status of Multi-National Military Implementation Force, paragraphs 8, 15, and 16.

20 Christopher Hill briefing, Ohrid, Macedonia, July 1999.

21 See Ian Black, James Meek and Ian Traynor, 'Russia and China lead International Protests', *The Guardian*, 26 March 1999

22 Conversation with Russian foreign-policy analyst, Rhodes, Greece, June 1999.

23 Transcript of the Plenary Session of the Russian State Duma, 3 February 1999, cited in

Oksana Antonenko, 'Russia, NATO and European Security after Kosovo,' *Survival*, vol. 41, no. 4, Winter 1999–2000, p. 133.

[24] Oksana Antonenko, in *ibid.*

[25] See Prime Minister Tony Blair, 'Doctrine of the International Community', speech delivered in Chicago on 22 April 1999; available at: http://www.number-10.gov.uk/public/info/index.html; and President Clinton, television address, 24 March 1999, published in *Washington Post*, 25 March 1999, p. A34.

[26] 'Nato, British Leaders Allege "Genocide"', CNN (March 29, 1999); also statements from Prime Minister Tony Blair (April 1999) in House of Commons and *Chicago Tribune* (23 April 1999). See also statements from President Clinton to the UN General Assembly (21 September 1999), Ambassador-at-large David J. Scheffer (17 December 1999 and 7 April 1999).

[27] The Hague Tribunal estimated in November 1999, based on data compiled from Western intelligence sources, eyewitness accounts and evidence taken from surviving family members, that there were 11,334 bodies at 529 sites. See statement of International Criminal Tribunal for the former Yugoslavia (ICTY) Chief Prosecutor Carla del Ponte, 10 November 1999, and Michael Ignatieff, 'Counting Bodies in Kosovo', *New York Times*, 21 November 1999, p.15.

[28] Christopher Hill briefing, Ohrid, Macedonia, July 1999.

[29] Adam Roberts, 'NATO's "Humanitarian War" over Kosovo', *Survival*, vol. 41, no. 3, Autumn 1999, p. 114.

[30] Benjamin S. Lambeth, *NATO's Air War for Kosovo: A Strategic and Operational Assessment* (Santa Monica: RAND, 2001), especially pp. 128–136.

[31] An excellent account by Ivo H. Daalder and Michael E. O'Hanlon makes clear that the Clinton administration, during the week that the war ended, had all but decided for a ground invasion – and that the decision would have been endorsed by the NATO allies. This likelihood was conveyed to Milosevic by Russian envoy Viktor Chernomyrdin on 27 May. *Winning Ugly: NATO's War to Save Kosovo* (Washington DC: The Brookings Institution, 2000), pp.155–161. On the impact in Moscow, see Appendix 30, Select Committee Report (23 May 2000), House of Commons – Foreign Affairs – Appendices to the Minutes of Evidence, Memorandum submitted by Oleg Levitin.

[32] James P. Thomas, *The Military Challenges of Transatlantic Coalitions*, Adelphi Paper 333 (Oxford: Oxford University Press for the IISS, 2000), p. 47.

[33] 'Moral Combat: NATO at War', BBC2 Documentary written and presented by Alan Little, broadcast on 12 March 2000.

[34] *Ibid*

[35] This insight was suggested to me by Christopher Greenwood.

[36] An excellent first-hand account of these bureaucratic battles comes from the then SACEUR, General Wesley K. Clark, *Waging Modern War* (New York: Public Affairs, 2001).

[37] 'The European Rapid Reaction Force', in *The Military Balance 2001–2002* (Oxford University Press for the IISS), pp. 283–291.

[38] Anthony Forster and William Wallace, 'What is NATO for?', *Survival*, vol. 43, no. 4, Winter 2001–02.

Chapter 4

[1] This is not to suggest that Serbs were anything but enraged about NATO's bombing of their country.

[2] For this author's own grim prediction, Dana H. Allin, 'Borders Are Bound to Change…', *Wall Street Journal Europe*, 1 April, 1999, p. 10.

[3] Rubin himself has described this relationship in 'Moral Combat: NATO at War', BBC2 documentary written and presented by Alan Little, broadcast 12 March 2000.

[4] Dana Priest, 'A Decisive Battle That Never Was', *Washington Post*, 19 September 1999, p. A1.

[5] 'What Happened to the KLA?', ICG Balkans Report 88 (3 March 2000), p. 20.

[6] 'Peace in Presevo: Quick Fix or Long-term Solution?', International Crisis Group, Balkans Report 116 (10 August 2001), available at www.crisisweb.org.

[7] 'President Clinton's Remarks at Portrait Unveiling of Former Secretary of State Warren Christopher', The White House Office of the Press Secretary, 30 March 1999, at http://clinton4.nara.gov/WH/New/html/19990330-1371.html; R. Jeffrey Smith, 'Specter of Independent Kosovo Divides U.S., European Allies', *The Washington Post*, 28 September 1999; Joseph Fitchett, 'Clinton Tilt on Kosovo Worries Europeans', *International Herald Tribune*, 1 October 1999.

[8] Author conversation, Washington DC, April 2000.

[9] Kosovars have been perfectly consistent in rejecting this solution. As Rugova put it in early 1996, 'Yugoslavia was destroyed, and with it, our ability to remain'. Author/ICOB interview, Pristina, January 1996.

[10] A seven-member presidency, with one mandated seat for a Serb and a second for another minority, will elect a 'president' who in turn will nominate a prime minister.

[11] See Alexandros Yannis, 'Kosovo Under International Administration', *Survival*, vol. 43, no. 2, Summer 2001, p.44.

[12] *Strategic Survey 2000–01* (Oxford: Oxford University Press for the IISS, 2001).

[13] Framework Agreement, concluded at Ohrid, Macedonia, signed at Skopje, Macedonia on 13 August 2001.

[14] *Ibid.*

[15] Author interviews, Washington DC, October 1998.

[16] Briefings by President Milo Djukanovic and other Montenegrin officials.

[17] For an excellent audit of these problems across a range of post-war administrations, see Richard Caplan, *A New Trusteeship? The International Administration of War-torn Territories*, Adelphi Paper 341 (Oxford: Oxford University Press for the IISS, 2002).

[18] For a critique of the election and detailed summary of results, see *Elections in Bosnia and Herzegovina*, International Crisis Group Report, 1996, www.crisisweb.org.

[19] Deputy High Representative Michael Steiner Conversation

with author, Aspen, Colorado, July 1997. See also Carl Bildt, 'Europe and Bosnia: Lessons of the Past and Paths for the Future', Speech of the High Representative, The Hague, 27 May 1997, at http://www.ohr.int/speeches/s970527a.htm

[20] *Ibid.*

[21] The city of Sarajevo, for example, was punished in summer 1998 with EU and USAID sanctions because of inadequate minority returns; but they were compensated with money from Islamic donors. Author interviews, Sarajevo, July 1998.

[22] Author interview, Pristina, July 2000.

[23] Author interviews, Sarajevo, July 2000.

[24] Michael R. Gordon, 'Bush Would Stop US Peacekeeping in Balkan Fights', *New York Times*, 21 October 2000.

[25] At a roundtable with Slav and Albanian members of the Macedonian parliament, weeks after Bush's inauguration and weeks before the outbreak of fighting near Tetevo, every Macedonian participant said he or she expected, and feared, a US withdrawal. Meeting at IISS Arundel House, London, February 2001.

[26] Author/ICOB interviews, Istanbul, Ankara, Athens, and Saloniki, October/November, 1995; see also Tindemans *et al.*, *Unfinished Peace*, pp. 132–136.

[27] Marta Dassú and Nicholas Whyte, 'America's Balkan Disengagement?', *Survival*, vol. 43, no. 4, Winter 2001–2.

[28] Oleg Levitin, 'Inside Moscow's Kosovo Muddle', *Survival*, vol. 42, no.1, Spring 2000.

Conclusion

[1] See Dana H. Allin, 'Unintended Consequences: Managing Kosovo Independence', in Dimitrios Triantaphyllou (ed.), *What Status for Kosovo?*, Chaillot Paper 50 (Paris: Institute for Security Studies, Western European Union, 2001), p.12.

[2] Author interviews, Pristina, July 2000.

[3] Ivo H. Daalder, 'Bosnia After SFOR: Options for Continued US Engagement', *Survival*, vol. 39, no. 4, Winter 1997–98, pp. 5–21.

[4] John Chipman, 'Director's Summing Up: Statement Made at IISS Annual Conference, The Strategic Implications of Terror in the Information Age', 15 September 2001, at www.iiss.org.